LETTERS ☆ FROM ☆ THE ☆ SAND

☆ THE LETTERS OF DESERT STORM AND OTHER WARS ☆

BY THE UNITED STATES POSTAL SERVICE

DESERT STORM VICTORY PARADE
PHOTO BY TERRY ASHE © TIME MAGAZINE

DEDICATION

This book was conceived by the United States Postal Service as a tribute to the American spirit as expressed so vividly in the letters to and from their loved ones by the men and women engaged in combat in the Persian Gulf. The same spirit runs through the letters retrieved from earlier conflicts. All point up the commonality and poignancy of spirit experienced by all soldiers in all wars.

Operation Desert Storm and Operation Desert Shield helped Americans everywhere rediscover the art of letter writing. The United States Postal Service is proud to have played a critical role in forging this vital link between those who served and their loved ones who could only wait and pray.

We dedicate "Letters from the Sand" to the brave men and women who responded so gallantly to this most recent call to duty and to their families and friends. We also remember those who served and did not return, such as John T. Boxler, a postal employee from Johnstown, Pennsylvania, who lost his life in this most recent hostile action.

Finally, I want to express my deep appreciation to the thousands of Americans who provided letters from relatives and friends. This made it possible to share the private thoughts and deep emotions of these men and women in uniform and to savor anew the strength and resilience of the American people.

Anthony M. Frank
Postmaster General

PUBLICATION NO. 91- 066741 (ISBN 96309552-0-X)

36USC 380

☆TABLE☆OF☆CONTENTS☆

☆ FOREWORD ☆

When the first shots were fired in the Persian Gulf War, they echoed throughout United States history. This was the fifth declared war in which the United States was involved. There also were numerous U.S. military actions other than declared wars in which the citizens of this nation have been called to arms to defend democracy at home or to protect it overseas.

The Persian Gulf conflict was a different kind of war. The United States did not "go it alone." Rather, it joined with the forces of many nations in a unified effort to oust the Iraqi invaders from Kuwait. This war also was a war without a surprise attack such as those common in most other wars. This time the United States and its Allies waited patiently, built up their forces, and gave the invaders a chance to retreat from Kuwait and prevent bloodshed.

This was a war fought in sand. Sand fouled the equipment, creating problems both at the front and in the back-up areas. Keeping equipment clean—from rifles to helicopters—was a constant activity. It is easy to imagine sand moving through an hourglass, each grain bringing the time of battle a bit closer.

The line had been drawn in the sand and the allied forces waited for the Iraqis to move back behind it and thus prevent war. The withdrawal did not come! The war did! The Americans and their Allies launched the attack, beginning the job for which they had trained and for which they had waited patiently over many months.

In each of its wars, Americans from all walks of life responded to the call. Members of the Reserve and National Guard, both young and old, male and female, were called on to set aside their civilian pursuits to stand shoulder to shoulder with their professional military counterparts.

What had been a normal lifestyle had to be altered to meet the needs of and the commitment to the nation. Evidence of the impact was easy to find in all parts of the country. Farmers stepped down from their plows, knowing they soon could be driving tanks. Technicians shut down their computers as they prepared to keep the automated machines of war ready to do their job. Mechanics wiped the grease from their hands, put away their tools, and began packing. Teachers left the classrooms, stopping to reassure their students that they would be back as soon as the battle was won.

Doctors, nurses, and other medical specialists packed their instruments and left to serve in medical units and hospitals in the field, as well as on hospital ships. In some families both the father and the mother were members of reserve units and both were called. They bid a hasty farewell to their children, not knowing when or if they would ever see them again.

Many of the recalled warriors found their patriotism taxed further by the losses they suffered when they gave up their civilian salaries and tried to survive on their military pay.

In short order these citizen heroes were on their way to fight yet another battle, a battle which would leave bloodstained evidence of their sacrifice on the battle flags of their units.

While the sacrifice of those called was great, there also was sacrifice, concern, and prayer on the part of the families left behind. They watched newscasts by the hour. Television brought the war into American living rooms almost as fast as the shots were being fired. One four-year old waited patiently for his parents to leave the TV so he could watch cartoons. As he tired of waiting he asked, "When is the war show going to end?"

Fears and prayers for the safety of loved ones were shared not only by their family members back home, but by most Americans. Yellow ribbons brightened the trees and mailboxes as families and friends waited to be reunited with their loved ones.

If one factor had to be isolated and identified as the key to keeping morale high in the units in the war zone, it would be the letters exchanged between the troops in the field and the families back home.

These letters tell the story of war in a way more eloquent than any fiction writer could imagine. They tell of happiness at the prospect of returning home. They joke about the quality and quantity of the food they eat. They grieve for their comrades who have fallen in battle. They tell of sharing fear and friendship in battle and of the love they have for the folks waiting at home. Some reflect the resentment they feel against protesters back home. Others tell of their efforts to help children orphaned by the war and abandoned by the community.

All of the letters both to and from the war zones show the sincerity of the writers. Sometimes the writing was almost illegible. It is easy to imagine these letters being written with the paper pressed against a field pack or a stone as the writer bridged the gap between "over here" and "over there." These letters were not written for publication or for a television show. They are an honest effort to reflect war as seen through the eyes of the participants. And, they do it admirably.

Although this book covers many wars, it recognizes the common thread that runs through them, spanning the chasm of time and reflecting the awful loneliness that is war.

The importance of letters to men and women in the armed forces is summed up beautifully in the book "Dear America: Letters Home From Vietnam," edited by Bernard Edelman. A paragraph from the foreword to "Dear America" is reproduced here with the permission of the New York Vietnam Veterans Memorial Commission. They were written by Bill Broyles who served in Vietnam.

"With the possible exception of his rifle, nothing was more important to an American in Vietnam than his mail. In 1969 I was a Marine lieutenant commanding a platoon in the mountains west of Da Nang. Twice a week a helicopter would bring out the red mail sack...the squad leaders would pass out the mail to their men....each package would be shaken ...if it contained cookies or other edibles, etiquette required that it be immediately shared and given a rating. Men who received consistently low ratings were encouraged to instruct their correspondents to improve the quality of their mailings. Everyone knew who was getting mail and who wasn't, who was having trouble at home, whose girl friend was trying to let him down gently. It was a special time, private also communal."

In letters, in pictures, in poetry and song, the story of war is told. Since it is told best by those who took part, every effort has been made to hold editing to a minimum.

Space, research, and time limitations made it necessary to deal only with those wars beginning with the Civil War and continuing through the Persian Gulf War.

Battlefield letters have an eloquence that blurs the spelling errors or improper grammatical construction. The letters are the true chronology of war recorded by those who came, those who fought, and those who died to preserve liberty. They wrote about what they saw, what they thought, and what they believed. Their letters are part of the history of our country in its most troubled times. There is nothing to be added that would improve the story or the telling of it.

1991

⋆ DESERT ⋆ STORM ⋆

When the United States went to war to free Kuwait, it stirred a wave of patriotism unlike any seen in recent years. This was a popular war, fought for a just cause, and the people wanted the service men and women to know that their effort was supported and appreciated. One of the most effective ways to do this was to encourage people all over the country to write to "any serviceman" and thank him or her for their sacrifice.

The idea caught on and thousands of mail sacks were part of the supply shipments to the troops. People wrote to people they didn't know and didn't know what to expect in reply. Many friendships and at least a few romances were among the results that tumbled from those mailbags.

Sometimes the letter writers got an unexpected bonus. Look what happened to a letter from one class in Vineland, N J.

President and Mrs. George Bush visited the troops during the Thanksgiving holiday.

Joan Bergamo is a fourth-grade teacher at Marie D. Durand School in Vineland. Her class wrote many letters to service personnel in the Persian Gulf. To their surprise and delight, they got a reply from the Chairman of the Joint Chiefs of Staff, Colin L. Powell. He felt it was worth his time to reply to the 16 questions they posed for him.

"Dear Students. Thank you for your letters, your poems, your pictures and your drawings. And, most of all, thank you for your kind words and for your overwhelming support of our men and women in the armed forces.

"I counted 16 questions! So let me see if I can answer them for you.

"(1) It is exciting and a great challenge to be President Bush's top military advisor.

"(2) I feel very fortunate to be the son of Jamaican immigrants. My parents were two very wonderful people who imparted to me a set of values that I treasure.

"(3) I am married. My wife's name is Alma. I have three children. Michael, my son, is in law school at Georgetown University. Through Michael and his wife I have a grandson Jeffrey. My daughter, Linda, is an actress living in New York City. My daughter Annemarie is a student at William and Mary College.

"(4) Yes, I am very glad the war is over.

"(5) I enjoy being a general because I get to work with troops anywhere. It always raises my morale to meet with men and women of our armed forces.

"(6) I live in Quarters No. 6 at Fort Myer, Virginia. From my house I can see the Washington Monument, the Lincoln Memorial, the Jefferson Memorial and other Washington sights.

"(7) I was in Vietnam twice, once in 1962-63 and again in 1968-69.

"(8) My birthday is 5 April and I am 54 years old.

"(9) I did not want the war with Iraq to start, but when Iraq invaded Kuwait Mr. Saddam Hussein started the war. The United Nations and the Coalition gave him over 5 months to stop the war and to withdraw his army. When he did not withdraw, we made him withdraw.

"(10) I was awarded the Purple Heart when I was wounded by a booby trap in Vietnam.

"(11) I was appointed by President Bush to be the 12th Chairman of the Joint Chiefs of Staff and I took office on October 1, 1989. I then became the principal military advisor to the President, the Secretary of Defense, the National Security Council and other national leaders.

"(12) Yes, this was the first time General Schwarzkopf and I worked directly together in a war, although both of us fought in Vietnam as well.

"(13) I don't have a favorite color or food — there are so many of both that I like, I'd be hard pressed to pick only one.

"(14) My best hobby is rebuilding old cars.

"(15) The highest general in our Armed Forces is the Chairman of the Joint Chiefs of Staff. And, yes, I think being a general is exciting, challenging, and it gives you an opportunity to work with some outstanding people.

"(16) Yes, General Schwarzkopf is a superb gentleman. I've always enjoyed working with him.

"Now that I've answered your questions, let me ask a favor of each one of you. Study hard, do your homework, be kind to one another, and always remember that in America your dreams can come true. If you are prepared, if you get a good education, if you work hard, you have unlimited opportunities available to you.

"Thank you again for writing and for your wonderful support of our men and women in uniform. Your cards, letters, cookies and packages really meant a lot to those brave Americans in the Gulf.

Sincerely,
Colin L. Powell,
Chairman, Joint Chiefs of Staff."

"Thank you for the recent package you sent us. It means a great deal to know you are thinking of us. We posted the Christmas card you sent in our Coordination Center so that everyone could enjoy it.

"You may have studied about the Middle East in your classes. The cities and cultures here are quite different than back home. The weather is also quite different, especially in the winter. It is very warm and dry, and you can usually be comfortable wearing shorts and T shirts.

"Yes, you can see camels here; they even have camel races, much like we have horse races back home. The people here speak Arabic, yet write their numbers using Indian characters. We speak English, yet write our numbers using Arabic characters. Luckily, many people here speak English, and we are learning some Arabic."

Col. Thomas F. Bliss, commander 552nd AWACW Deployed, also provided a history lesson in his thank-you note for a package to Girl Scout Troop 4504 in Morgantown, WV.

"By the way, did you know Arabic is written and read from right to left instead of the way we write from left to right? They also read their books from the back to the front. Seems backwards doesn't it? But, to them, our way is backwards.

"The environment is very hard for someone who is not from here to deal with. There are very few flowers or trees or anything green for that matter. It is all brown and sand every place. Some of the rich people tend to try and grow trees and flowers. I guess the beauty of trees and flowers is the same to all cultures. So next time you go outside and smell flowers or see a tree, don't take it for granted because not everyone in the world can enjoy scenery like we can in the United States."

Air Force Capt. Arvella Gardner, 7 ACCS, added a history lesson when she responded to a letter from Nancy Bennett's third-grade class in Southampton, NY.

"Kuwait is the diminutive of the Arabic "Kut" meaning a fortress built near water. Most of Kuwait consists of waterless desert which is undulating and gravelly.

"...There is something about the harshness and desolation of the desert that brings one's thoughts toward God. Perhaps it is the solitude of the desert, especially at night under a big dark blue sky illuminated by more stars than you have ever seen, that declares the presence of God as the creator the heavens and the earth. And, perhaps, it is also dwelling in a dry and thirsty land which causes one's spiritual awareness to heighten.

"Read Psalms chapter 63 which speaks of thirsting for God in the desert. It is important to note that many men of God in both the Old and the New Testaments, including Christ Himself, were called by God into the desert for a time of preparation and testing. The desert sand forges men of spiritual strength."

David C. White is a captain in the Army and an attorney. He wrote in response to a letter from Ria Wright which she wrote as part of a ninth-grade English project. He provided both a history and philosophy lesson to the class.

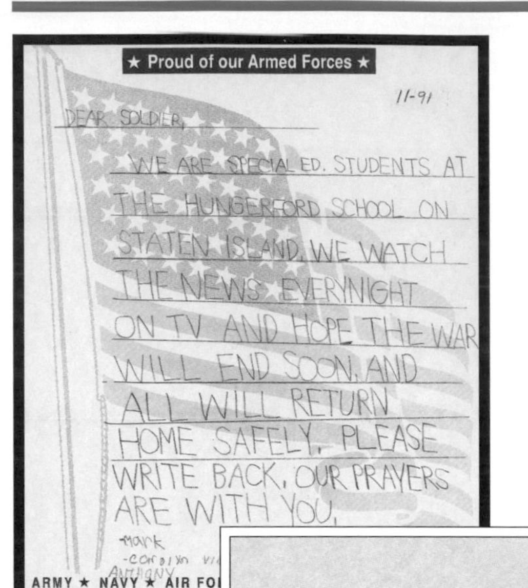
★ Proud of our Armed Forces ★

11-91

DEAR SOLDIER,

WE ARE SPECIAL ED. STUDENTS AT THE HUNGERFORD SCHOOL ON STATEN ISLAND, WE WATCH THE NEWS EVERYNIGHT ON TV AND HOPE THE WAR WILL END SOON, AND ALL WILL RETURN HOME SAFELY, PLEASE WRITE BACK, OUR PRAYERS ARE WITH YOU,

-Mark
-Carolyn
Anthony

ARMY ★ NAVY ★ AIR FO

"Dear Class: Thanks for a pretty card and keep praying for me on a safe return home. My name is Lawford Demargo Domineck. I'm from Baton Rouge, Louisiana.

"I hope all of you will write me back. I've been in the army four years. All of you really touched my heart. Keep me in your prayers. OK, please write back. A far away friend, Cpl Domineck."

Students in Ms. P. Cognata's Special Ed Class at Hungerford School, Staten Island, NY, were thrilled when they received this letter from Cpl. Lawford Demargo Domineck of Co. D, 269th Engr. Bn. He was equally touched by their letter.

"Dear Sgt. Ward,

"This is your daughter so don't think it's someone in my class. I wish you would come home soon I cry every night when we pray.

"First it was James, now it's me. Everyone is asking me about you. Today is January 29. I showed the sand from Saudi Arabia that you gave me.

"We pray for you every night. I guess my friends are writing more than I am, well maybe not. Our Girl Scout troop is waiting for you to come to take some mail. The weather is nice and cool. Is the weather OK up there?"

"The feeling of freedom touches us every day and as you reach your teenage years and beyond, you will gain a higher knowledge of it, at the same time removing most of the limits you have now. The food you eat, the clothes you choose to wear, the TV programs you watch, and even the school books you learn from are possible only through the freedom we have worked for throughout this country's entire history.

"How does that explain Desert Storm and what is happening right now? Well, think of the little country Kuwait as our friend, and Iraq Saddam Hussein is acting like a bully. Then, think of the United States as the authority figure, like parents, a teacher, principal, maybe even a police officer. The bully is generally stronger, and pushes the little person around, taking freedom away, in this case through an invasion.

"Our country, as keepers of world peace, tries to limit or take away that strength of the bully, and keep them apart from each other, hence the bombing of Iraqi planes, military bases and their fighting people. The US does this with their military forces, which is where I fit in in the Air Force.

"Now, fighting for peace is very confusing to some, but when you realize that five months of talking and pleading was getting nowhere, and the blocking of food and money supply lines didn't faze them, we knew the stubborness would continue."

MSgt. Steve Ward wrote a letter to his daughter's fourth grade class while he was serving in the Persian Gulf area. The first batch of replies he got included one from his daughter who wanted to be sure he knew her letter was special.

"Hello! My name is Senior Airman Fernando Casilla. Today I received your letters from Des Plaines. Even though they were addressed to the Army boys over here, I am very glad they were given to me. All of you are a great group and I thank each one of you for including your links of friendship and true American support. All of you are my new friends.

"Being in the military is a demanding and sometimes difficult duty, as many of you already know. But, the reward is priceless. Our American veterans, prisoners of past wars, those who have been missing in action, and our brothers, the unknown soldiers have, in days gone by, forged the freedom of our great home, America.

"They will not have their work, and their fight forgotten. Because we enjoy liberty and peace in the United States, I and my fellow service members continually do our work with much pride and enthusiasm. Helping to preserve our nation's security is an honorable and noble opportunity."

The eighth-grade class at Chippewa Junior High School, Des Plaines, IL, addressed their letter to any soldier. It came into the hands of Senior Airman Fernando Casilla, assigned to Air Force aerial refueling of KC135s.

"Dear Col. Petri,

"How are you? Is this your first time to fight? Here are some quotes. 'Speak softly and carry a big stick,' Theodore Roosevelt. 'The art of war is simple. Find out where the enemy is and get him as soon as you can. Strike at him as hard as you can and keep moving.' Ulysses S. Grant, and 'The only thing we have to fear is fear itself' Franklin D. Roosevelt.

"The reason why I chose this is because you probably need all the confidence you can get.

"Love, Nikki Browning."

Col. Jack Petrie, MEF-G-3 (ARCENT), got a chuckle out of this bundle of advice from student Nikki Browning of Smyrna, TN.

Friendships and romances occasionally bloom under rather interesting circumstances. This is what happened to a fourth-grade teacher in Albany, WI. As a school assignment Rochelle Lerch had her class write letters to servicemen from the area who were serving in the Persian Gulf. MM3 Lonnie Van Dusen, aboard the aircraft carrier John F. Kennedy, wrote back promptly. Ms. Lerch sent him a thank-you note for the rapid reply. Soon the sailor was writing a steady stream of letters to the teacher.

When he returned home in April, Ms. Lerch invited him to visit her class and share his Desert Storm experiences. A real story-book ending: He fell in love with the teacher. They will be married in December.

"In your letter you asked if we were brave. Well, I've been in the Marine Corps for 14 years and have done many harrowing things from parachuting from an airplane to climbing mountains, and each time I was full of fear. My heart was going a million miles an hour, sweating and hoping my insurance was paid up. We rely on our training and our brains to get us through, but the fear is still there.

"Maybe it's sort of the way you felt when you had to get up in front of a class and read or recite your poem. Were you scared?

"My Mom and Dad taught me when I was about your age that it's OK to feel scared. But, if you're prepared and your task isn't foolhardy then, you just say a little prayer to God to watch over you and then give it your best.

"And, if in the very end you fail and can't try again, than you can walk away and say you gave it your best shot. That, in itself is an accomplishment! I guess that is what brave it all about, it's what we do with fear."

Marine Staff Sgt. Lawrence N. Grutek, Jr., wrote to the students at Margaret Sheehy Elementary School in Merced, CA. He gave them a lesson on dealing with fear.

Magdalena Scheff of Fort Lauderdale, FL, shares this poem written by her 12-year-old niece Julie Van Vranken to her father James Van Vranken, an E-4 in the Coast Guard, while he was on duty in the Persian Gulf.

"My Dad he left just hours ago,
when he'll be back I do not know,
he said don't worry cause I'll be fine,
you are important to me because your mine.

"My Dad he left just days ago,
my nights are long my days are slow,
I received a letter today in the mail,
he said that he is ready to sail.

"My Dad he left just weeks ago,
been gone so long here comes the snow,
he is over there with the Coast Guard
being without him is very hard.

"My Dad he left just months ago
my gosh where did all the time go.
It's hard to watch the news at night,
seeing the war is a great deal of fright.

"Well, now he's been gone a very long while
I see his picture it brings me a smile.
On a clear blue sky outshines the moon,
I think of the Soldiers.
PLEASE COME HOME SOON."

The story of the Desert Storm War is told from many angles. Like a patchwork quilt it is composed of pieces of information that are combined to paint a complete picture. Some of the letters give frightening accounts of combat operations. Others tell of situations that turned out to be more exciting than dangerous. In this letter Staff Sgt. Michael B. Wichman of the 826th Ordnance Company tells his father, Ben Wichman of Appleton, WI, about his encounter with an Iraqi tank.

"Once we got near downtown Kuwait City we really began to see some interesting sights. The first thing we saw were the Iraqi tanks. There we were, driving down the expressway when suddenly we noticed something in the highway ahead of us —a tank, a big tank, a big Iraqi tank!

"We slowed down then we stopped to take a look at it. There it was, a Soviet made main battle tank, just sitting in the middle of the highway - empty! It was fully loaded, not a shell had been fired out of it. The Iraqis had abandoned it when the Allies started the ground offensive. All they were interested in was getting out of the way, and a tank was too slow and too big a target so they just left it. We saw approximately 12 Iraqi tanks left like this."

"My first combat mission occurred this afternoon. I was a HARM (High Speed Anti Radiation Missile) shooter in support of a pre-planned strike mission well into Iraqi territory. I was obviously a bit apprehensive but I knew what I had to do and was well trained to do it. I would like to go into details, but much of it is top secret and if I did I would have to kill you when I got home. Just kidding, of course.

"To keep this declassified I will tell you about the generalities. The HARM is a very expensive missile ($750,000 each) which is designed to hone in on the emissions from the surface to air missile radars.

"I shot my first two HARMs today to take out the SAM sites in the target area before the strikers (bombers) got close enough to get shot at. None of the strikers were shot at so I guess I accomplished my mission. The highly mobile sites may have moved from the target area which means my HARMs impacted terra firma without hitting anything.

"It gets rather busy in a single seat strike fighter when working your air to air radar looking for the threat, ensuring you're on your navigation route and timing, setting up your computer for delivering your weapons and looking out of the cockpit to stay in proper formation with the package searching for SAMs and enemy aircraft. The Hornet is a great jet and one can accomplish their mission if they have their stuff in one bag and a little luck.

"I think I know the Marine F/A 18 pilot flying with the Navy who was shot down today. I try not to dwell on it. The possibility of getting shot down or killed is very real although we did very well today considering the number of sorties launched today. I hope we continue to decimate the Iraqis and send a message to the world that they better think twice before waking the sleeping giant."

Carolynne Seeman, Bethesda, MD, got a close up view of the war in a letter from her nephew USMC Marine Capt. Tim Royston of the Third Marine Air Wing as he described his first combat mission. Before the war ended he had flown 30 sorties.

This letter to Aleta C. Beaver from her brother Capt. Alan Cameron of the Army's First Armored Division describes the fighting and the refugees.

"The fighting between the Iraqi army and the rebels has gotten so vicious that people are coming to us from all directions. Behind U.S. lines is the only place in the country where people aren't killing each other so we've become a sort of sanctuary.

"Each day thousands of refugees stream through the checkpoint and it seems that everyone of them has a hole in them somewhere.

"The women and children, of course, are the worst to see. On the first day a little girl of about six died of malnutrition at the point, while another woman gave birth. Everyone else had wounds or burns and hadn't eaten in a couple of days.

"The desire to help now is greater than that to destroy ever was and it's a shame we can't do more for them. The most critically wounded we evac to our own hospitals and we patch up the rest, but it seems that the biggest part of our aid comes in the food and water we give away. We can't get it to the front fast enough."

"I forgot what a pain it is to do wash by hand... very busy with this end building bunkers and driving gear north. We are finally getting a tent with one light bulb. We stole the light bulb and the generator.

"All the gear we get we steal from the Army. The USMC will never change.

"I saw many oil wells this a.m. on the road back. Besides the wells all we saw was sand and a few camels. We rode a bus this morning with a sign saying 'all women must ride in the back of the bus.'"

Little nuisance problems get magnified when they are combined with all the other inconveniences in an assignment to the desert. CWO S. S. Baehren related a few in this letter to his wife, Deb Baehren of Toledo, OH.

Mrs. Vickey Lyden of Pompano Beach, FL, got a vivid description of the early days of the war from her son, Army Capt. David Doyal.

"The war, as you know, started on 24 February, but we did not cross the Iraqi border until the morning of the 25th. Almost immediately upon doing so though my unit started collecting POWs. By day's end not a shot had been fired but we had taken 300 Iraqi prisoners.

"The next day the rest of the brigade continued moving forward while I commanded a group of soldiers whose job it was to fix all the vehicles and tanks that had broken down to that point. So, quite suddenly, I was responsible for the lives of some 20 people. ....the enemy had largely fled. For four days we sat in the Iraqi desert fixing things and trying to stay out of trouble. When we finally rejoined our unit in Kuwait, I found I had been nominated for a bronze star.

"Here in Kuwait we are occupying a piece of desert formerly held by the Iraqis. The area is littered with several hundred bombed out tanks and artillery pieces. The shells of unexploded bombs are everywhere. Miraculously, my brigade got through the war without a single soldier killed. On the other side, however, we destroyed more than a division of Saddam's supposedly elite Republican Guards.

"The war has really taken its toll on this tiny country. Besides all the obvious damage I already told you about, the environment has really taken a beating.

"Just today it was pitch black at about 2:30 in the afternoon. It seems that the weather was just right not to dissipate the incredible volume of smoke from the burning oil fields to our north and south. It was one of the most eerie things I have ever experienced."

Dr. (Maj.) Michael Fishkin of the 142nd Medical Company (Clearing) kept a journal while he was in the war zone. The following three excerpts are from his journal.

"I'm glad I am the ranking officer. Everyone looks to me for stability during the attacks. I'm scared also, but knowing they are watching gives me the courage to continue.

"You cannot imagine the feeling of loneliness and vulnerability we have. We have no lights, the camp is dark and you lie in your suit and mask waiting for the all clear to sound. The sound of the valves in the gas masks is all you hear. You see nothing. Flashlight batteries are in short supply so we keep them off until they are truly needed."

"All is well. Morale is still high. We seem to have a sense of mission.

"I must say, however, that I have developed a reputation of coming up with equipment and supplies no one else can get. If it's not tied down and no one is looking, it disappears. It's great being a major. I have almost as much power as a nurse back home."

"As we played ball a huge convoy passed on the horizon. It stretched for miles and was heading into Harm's Way.

"As I watched the convoy I thought of the old caravans that used to travel these same routes. The only difference is now we have mechanized vehicles instead of camels."

"I am a U.S. Army chaplain stationed at King Fahad National Guard Hospital in Riyadh, Saudi Arabia. I personally want to thank you for your note of appreciation for our service members. Your little note made its way to our burn unit somehow while I was on duty.

"One young Army private who was severely burned on over 30% of his upper body had his day brightened as I read your Valentine card to him. He is unable to speak and will soon be airlifted to Germany. He expressed his appreciation for your message by giving me a thumbs up. He wanted to tell me something by blinking his eyes rapidly. After a few questions I got out of him the request for me to write to you and to say 'thank you' for your card. His name is Noel and he is from one of the Pacific islands.

"As soldiers commited to freeing Kuwait, we are thankful to a grateful nation back home who have not forgotten us. We love you. If we can keep our next generation free from tyrants and dictators like Hussein, then we feel this was a just cause."

o matter how badly they were wounded servicemen still had a deep appreciation for mail and the people who sent it. Chaplain (Maj.) Donald W. Myers, 382nd Field Hospital, wrote Martha Tucker, Bellmore, NY, about one such soldier and his reaction to a letter.

"I pray every night for this thing to get over with ASAP. Two nights ago we lost another aircraft and both pilots were killed. Last night we lost an F-18. That pilot also was killed. We had a ceremony today on the flight deck for them. It was so sad, I looked around and everyone had tears in their eyes (including me). It feels like I've lost three friends and I don't even know them. But I'll tell you one thing, they were my shipmates and damn good fighter pilots who were willing to die for their country just as I am willing to die for America. God Bless the USA!

"All pilots left behind a child so they set up a trust fund for them. I gave $200 because I thought it was something that I was obligated to do, and I feel good for doing it."

One of the most traumatic effects of war is the impact the death of a comrade has on his surviving friends. This letter was sent to Glen and Debbie Bright by their son E-3 Erick A. Bright while serving aboard the Aircraft Carrier USS Theodore Roosevelt.

"Everyone is working around the clock and although it has only been three days since our first strike it seems like it's been three weeks.

"I finally got put on the night shift to try and build up some night time for my airline pilot license and it turns out my first sortie was the night it all started.

"I came in to brief up and got the word from our commanders the war was about to start. As you can imagine, my blood pressure went right through the roof. I was airborne when the balloon went up. It was the worst feeling in the world not knowing what to expect and I am not afraid to say that I was scared to death. My adrenaline was really pumping and after it was all over my body came down hard. I could hardly get out of the jet. I was more physically exhausted than I ever have been before.

"I can't tell you much more about it other than that what we are doing is really helping our campaign. I try to focus on that fact alone and it helps me mentally prepare for the next mission. I don't doubt that our principles are right, it's just hard to accept the fact that thousands of people will be killed before it is all over. It's also hard to believe that some people really get a kick out of this. You have to have confidence, but you don't have to enjoy it."

The fear suffered by an Air Force pilot on his first combat mission was described in this letter from Capt. Chris McDonald to his mother Mrs. Dorothy F. McDonald of Charlotte, NC.

"...the deadline had passed...the time had come of age. I went to sleep and the next thing I remembered was a guy running through my tent yelling that the war had started (this was at 3 a.m.).

"It was strange. The whole camp was a flurry of commotion. My troops all came to my hooch, all fully dressed. They didn't know what to expect, but in their own minds, they were ready for 'war.' They all had questions about what to do. I suppose they all came to me because SSgt Hartman is the one that 'has the answer.'

"Of course, I am new to war also, but I gave them the most reasonable answer that I could muster. I said 'go back to sleep. Our mission starts at 0700 and that's when you have to be at your best.' There was nothing more said. All left and things got quiet.

"I don't mean to sound nonchalant, but if I was falling to pieces they would do the same. They saw my determination and felt my confidence and that is what they needed."

A friend gave Laura Opfer of Bothwell, WA, a list of service people in the Persian Gulf who would enjoy receiving a letter. She selected the name of Staff Sgt. John Hartman. She eventually received 25 letters from him and they became good friends. She hoped that someday they might have a chance to meet. That hope was realized when she flew to Hawaii to meet him. In his first letter to her he described the opening day of the ground war.

Sgt. Michael A. Freitas of the 101st Airborne Division tried to ease the fears of his mother, Judy Mims of Carthage, MO, as he described injuries he suffered in a helicopter crash.

"I'm writing this from my hospital bed somewhere in Saudi Arabia. The Blackhawk helicopter I was on crashed shortly after take-off on 16 February. It smashed my left foot. Somehow nothing was broken. It looked pretty bad, all purple and swollen. I can move it a little more every day. I can even walk using crutches now.

"I'll give you all the details. A wind storm had been going on for about 25 hours. We had my whole squad plus some more people for a total of 15 passengers with all equipment. We were on our way to join our battalion deep in Iraq. We were packed like sardines.

"I was on the left door because I had to scope at the landing zone when we landed. Well, we didn't make it that far. The aircraft lifted off and got up to about 100 feet when it started slanting down toward the left. We knew something was up by the way it was going down but it all happened so fast that we couldn't do anything about it.

"The bird hit and the left wheel strut snapped and the helicopter partly rolled over to the left side. The ground ripped the door off and I hit the ground. I got dragged along from 10-20 meters before it completely stopped.

"I tried to get up but my foot was stuck between the ground and the bird. It seemed like forever but I pulled free and stood up.

"The rotor had hit the ground and splintered. I pulled out three guys and then everyone poured out. We started to run but I couldn't make it. A couple of my friends carried me to a collection point. Some medics arrived shortly and put a splint on my foot. It is the Alabama National Guard 109th Hospital. Four of us got hurt. All wounds were to the feet and legs area. That was about two days ago and now two are walking without crutches.

"I'm expecting a full recovery and should be walking unaided in a few days. I'll have to find another pair of pants though, they cut mine off."

"I've a lot of letters to write but I had to get this off my mind. Last night and today I've been hanging out in the surgery rooms of the hospital. Believe me when I say that the reality of war hit me in the face.

"...The one that really got me was this 18-year old. I just left the operating room and it was a terrible sight. I don't know how it happened but right above and below his right elbow was blown to mere pieces. The only thing holding his arm was one side of skin. They didn't think they were going to be able to save his arm, but they were going to try.

"What bothers me along with the fact that he is so young is that right before they put him out he said 'just so you save my arm.' I sure hope they save it.

"I'm back. I had to go to CMS where they keep the instruments to learn more about oral surgery. On my way I stopped by the surgery room and they were able to save that 18-year-old's arm.

"At least so far. No one knows what will happen to it when he leaves here. All I know is that he was pretty messed up and went thru hell."

Spec. Jody Johnson, a medical specialist in the U.S. Army, sent this chilling account of her duty day to her parents Mr. and Mrs. Pat Johnson in Red Oak, IA.

"I don't know what's gonna happen here. Working the front gate I'm walking around with a bullseye on. At nite it's like it glows and we stick out like a sore thumb. At work at night on the front gate myself and the other three members are serious targets.

"I just want you to know you have made the past four months go by pleasantly and it would have been a lot tougher if I hadn't been writing to you. Basically I'm saying thank you for everything you have done for me. I owe you a great deal.

"I'll tell you why I am writing this. I'm scared... Not working has given me a chance to think and now I am really scared. I mean not that anything is going to happen but God forbid it does I just want you to know over the past four months I have came to think of you as more than a friend. Much more.

"Remember in a previous letter when I said it seemed like I've known you more than three months. I wasn't kidding. I feel like I've known you all my life and have been growing fonder with each day that passes. I feel a deeper feeling other than friendship. Please don't think I am crazy because I am not. Do you think it is possible to actually 'fall' for someone never even met face to face?"

When Kelly Anne Kane of Haverstown, PA, wrote to "Dear Braveheart (any service member)" she says the recipient rapidly went from a pen pal to a good friend. These excerpts are from a letter received on Valentine's Day from A/1C Patrick Baessler in the Persian Gulf area. Miss Kane reports they have stayed in "close contact" since his return to the States.

"Thank you for the letters, cards and cookies! Sorry it has taken so long to respond - we have been in the thick of it in the northern Persian Gulf. Right now we are steaming back and forth in a mine field. I know it must sound kind of scary, but after six weeks of it up here it has become just another day.

"We don't expect to have a problem...but we are always prepared in case we do. There is much I could tell you about these six weeks, they seem like a lifetime. Now, a bag of sea stories that doesn't have a bottom is the biggest acquisition - all else in a 14-year career seems tame compared to this - and yet, this is tame.

"Compared to any conflict with a real power, our war here is probably all but over except for those pesky mines. Mines Never Surrender. We had to move away from our anchorage spot earlier today when a minesweeper told us he had a mine about 3/4 miles away!

"We have blown up a lot of floating mines. But, you cannot see the real ones moored beneath the water. We are mostly working to ensure day to day safety and survival. It is not over until it's over or until the fat lady sings."

The dangers encountered in moving through seas with mines in them proved a constant challenge for Lt. Cmdr. William E. Jackson, executive officer on the USS Curtis. He painted a verbal picture for his sister, Linda Ivey, of Groves, TX.

"Hi, my name is Bill. I'm in the Navy and I live on the Battleship Wisconsin. I work on the big guns inside the turrets. They are the biggest guns in the world. The bullets are six feet long and weigh one ton each. I shoot them over 20 miles onto the shores of Iraq and Kuwait to help protect our army and marines. We also shoot Iraq's missile launchers so they can't shoot at us.

"I hope you will never have to go to war. I hope this will be the last war anyone ever has to fight. I'm glad you wrote to me because I get pretty lonely out here since I am over 10,000 miles away from my family.

"I've got to go now since I am very busy. If you want I will send you a USS Wisconsin baseball cap. So write back and let me know. OK?"

When Jayne Lord of the Bronx, NY, wrote an "any soldier" letter, she was surprised to get a reply from a sailor, GMGSA William Beaulieu of the USS Wisconsin.

This letter was sent to Lt. Col. Allan B. Morris of Louisville, KY, from a young man he recruited for and shepherded through the Air Force Academy. Capt. R. Givens graduated in May 1990.

"It's very difficult to convey in words the emotions of being in combat. I'm sure, however, that this experience is a significant emotional event that will most certainly impact the rest of my life. I will now view life through the eyes of a combat veteran.

"Every day back in the US will be a problem free day from now on. I know now that if I can make it through a war I can make it through anything."

Long work days were common in Operation Desert Storm. Marine Sgt. Calvin M. Lucado wrote to his mother, Margaret Broughton of Wyandotte, MI, about his work and his hours on the job. He was serving in Saudi Arabia at the time.

"I work from 0100 in the morning to 1 p.m. in the afternoon. We work with a bunch of Royal Saudi Air Force personnel in our shop.

"We are pretty safe here because we have a shelter that goes four stories below ground level.

"My job has become a vital link to the pilots to bomb targets in Iraq and Kuwait and also to give results after the bombing takes place.

"The big worry here is the terrorist activity in Riyadh. We carry protection and wear flack jackets whenever we are outside.

"I've enclosed some Saudi money for the youngsters. The currency is measured in Riyals."

Some towns really went out of their way to keep in touch with servicemen from their area. One such town is Walhalla, ND. The town had 16 local men in the National Guard unit that was stationed in the Gulf. Mrs. John Hornung forwards some of the letters from the troops overseas and adds this note:

"For whatever reason I began to keep the clippings from our local paper, the Grand Forks Herald and one other newspaper. My husband nicknamed me the shredder. To date I have 21 folders, each containing one hundred pages of clippings. When our men finally get home they may be interested in looking at the clippings kept at our local library." Following are excerpts of two of the letters she received.

Spc. Chad Fraser wrote:

"We were very busy when the ground war began. We put out 840,000 gallons plus in the first 24 hours. Some officers say it was a feat never achieved before in the Army and will probably be a standing record for quite some time. It was nice to finally get some 'good' recognition."

Spc. Kevin Gapp wrote:

"We have a couple of pets now. One is a little puppy that we were given by a transportation company. He is a fat little mutt who lives off extra MREs. He usually makes his daily rounds through the tents looking for treats and attention. The other is an owl our maintenance section has. It was found caught in the concertina wire that surrounds the camps here. They named him 'patriot' and the dog 'scud.' I think the owl might have gone now though.

"Well I guess that is about all from paradise for now so I will sign off. Thank you for everything."

"I am not getting a suntan. I have known for years that the sun and I are not friends but recently I found out we were terrible enemies. I was out making sandbags with sun block on - spent from 8 a.m. to 4:30 p.m. in the blazing sun. Had my uniform on, long sleeves and gloves so the only area exposed was my face not covered by goggles. The next day I looked like the bride of Frankenstein, swollen, rash. So now I rarely go out except when it is necessary. And, if I do, I'm covered from head to toe. When people see my lily white skin they'll never believe I was in the desert.

"...We have been getting more POWs - walking skeletons - scared to death. Culturally they are shocked by the number of female officers ordering enlisted men around. Even the rare Arab soldier that comes in is shocked.

"I don't know if we are making a good or a bad impression on them. Thank God they aren't allowed back in the living quarters - they'd have a stroke with all the exposed skin."

This letter is from Maj. Josepha Altersitz, a nurse assigned to the 300th Field Hospital. She writes to Susie Hubbard, Pitman, NJ. These letters give a little insight into the living conditions and working areas of nurses assigned to the Gulf. She also shares some thoughts about prisoners of war.

"Momma and Daddy. Hey, how are things going? They're going fine here. As a matter of fact, this is turning into like a regular job. We're getting one day off a week and we're not working but 12 hours a day now. Besides being in the desert heat, I carry my M-16 and chemical gear. It is just like a regular job.

"I found out yesterday that we could call once a week. My day is Sunday. It was good to hear yall's voice the other day. It really did cheer me up. And then last night I got a lot of mail so I'm in a real good mood.

"Gollygum, I still say they should have had this thing during the baseball season. We could have been back in time to see football."

This letter was sent to Mrs. Sandra Harper of Lindale, GA, by her 19-year-old son, Amn. Scotty Harper, 363 TFW. His father, Herbert Harper, has been employed by the Postal Service for 21 years as a letter carrier and now as supervisor of delivery and collections.

"Those who have never been overseas could never know just how good America is. The freedom that everyone has and the opportunities. This is a land of ultra wealth and struggling poverty, with no middle class.

"A lot of reserve soldiers will have a healthy respect for the U.S. after this is over.

"Pray for us not that we are blessed in combat, but that we may find a quick and peaceful solution to the problem."

Humor is the medicine that preserves sanity when all else seems like madness. Spec. Kenneth Alan Russell of the 70th Ord. Bn. provides a sample in this letter to his mother, Mrs. Alana Arant of Charlotte, NC.

"Don't worry too much, Mom. My spirits are high and when bad news comes round my ears, eyes, nose are open and I am also watching my back. I am very alert. My thinking is very positive. I have a life to live and a family to be with. Someday I will have a family of my own to carry on my name. That means a lot to me.

"Thanks very much for the Nikes. They fit and feel good. I really do appreciate them so much. My feet are smiling so big when they get out of those boots and slip in those shoes."

Patriotism is a virtue that shines clear in many of the letters compiled in this volume. SWCS George M. Havash, a Navy CB, shared his thoughts with his mother, Helen C. Havash, of N. Huntingdon, PA.

This letter was received by Burk J. Boggs, a letter carrier from Manassas, VA, from his cousin, Larry A. Dawson, Jr., who was serving in Saudi Arabia. His letter, like many others, shows the deep concern felt for family members back home by troops stationed in the Gulf.

"Overall I would say that spirits, including my own, are generally high, but even in the bravest face there is always a shadow of apprehension just behind the eyes. I personally hope that the crisis can be resolved diplomatically and, if not, with as little bloodshed and grief for those involved as is humanly possible.

"The main concern for most of the Marines here is for the ones we left behind. We often talk about our families, and our worst dread is that our absence is causing discomfort for them.

"Comfort my mother and my brother. We are fine. We are safe and we are not afraid, for God is with us."

Connie Garrett of Carmi, IL, wrote, "My husband was coach of the Carmi-White County High School baseball team. Danny Starks was the second baseman. Only eight months later Pvt. Starks was in Saudi Arabia, his engineering battalion attached to the 24th Mech. Inf. Div. This excerpt is from a letter Danny sent in thanks for a food package."

"I wish I could just hear the soft crack of the fungo (bat) as the baseball bounds my way. I so gracefully and effortlessly swoop it up and throw swiftly to S. J. at first.

"I almost break down when I think about if I could just do that right now! Mr. Garrett, I promise that for at least one home game you'll hear someone yell, 'Get down lower on it and don't turn your head!' And, when you turn to look, it'll be me rooting your dawgs on. Oh, how joyous that day will be."

Staff Sgt. Douglas E. Jarvis Jr. was assigned to a mail unit in the Persian Gulf and he got to see the joy mail brought to his "customers." He wrote a letter to Connie Methven, Postmaster of Milton, WA. He included some unusual requests. What happened after that is worth telling.

"My name is Doug Jarvis. Normally I live in Milton but for now I live elsewhere. My job over here is to deliver the mail to the northern APOs. I, we, I should say, get an enormous sense of satisfaction out of what we do. We make people smile who otherwise would have nothing to smile about. I take back all those nasty remarks about my hometown mail carrier.

"The reason I am writing this is that I would like to have your support. There are two things I would like for my platoon (1) some U.S. Mail bumper stickers or hats or patches (2) for me I would like a Washington state flag. I want to bring a little bit of 'evergreen' to this dismal, sandy place. Whatever you can do will be appreciated. I miss my home. We are keeping your tradition alive, but now you must add 'sandstorms' to your motto."

A second letter from Sgt. Jarvis deals with what happened when he got the items he requested.

"Thank you for answering my letter. I think that we started something here. Word got around about my writing to you and now everyone is writing their postmasters.

"My CO sort of...well let's say he had some words with me about my new hat. While he was discussing my change to the uniform the battalion commander just happened to walk by and saw my hat. It seems that his daughter is stationed in Fort Lewis. Knowing that I was a reservist he asked if I was with the Postal Service as a civilian. Well, I told him how I wrote you and that "you all" wrote back and sent the hats. He thought that I showed initiative and it was a good example of support for the troops, great motivation!

"Well, to make a long story short...I can wear my official Tacoma Truck Rodeo hat as long as I am in the APO. My CO is a little miffed.

"We are still moving over 300,000 pounds of mail daily and they are projecting more. The good news is that we will be home by the 4th of July. See ya'all soon!"

Some of the most heartwarming letters to the troops in the Gulf came from little children writing to their parents. Lt. Cmdr. Lou Moxcey, USS Santa Barbara, got this touching message from his eight-year-old son, Ben.

"Dear Dad, I hope your fine becous I'm fine. Remember the three gold fish that I told you abuat they all dided.

"I hope your haveing fun. I hope the ingen and other gajets on your ship are running good.

"Have you seen any whales? Wil you have been to sea? Are you going to get anything from Egypt? Love Ben Moxcey."

Pfc. John Penrod was glad he paid attention in math class while a student at Harbor Fields High School, Green Lawn, Long Island, NY, the school he attended before he entered the military. He sent this letter back to his former classmates.

"Well anyway, here I am in the sands of Northern Saudi Arabia with my M1A1 Abrams Main Battle Tank. I'm the driver, which is a lot of fun. As a matter of fact, my high school graduation tassle is in hanging up in my driver's hole.

"You can thank the math department for me. It seems I'm the only one who can convert latitude and longitude into military grid coordinates. So now Bravo Company won't get lost any more. But, more importantly, it earned me a lot of Brownie points.

"I can only blame myself for being here. I volunteered twice to get here. I have what very few people my age have and that is a sense of patriotic duty. Maybe now some of my counterparts will get some idea of what that means.

"I could be making more working two shifts at Burger King and not have to worry about being shot at. So let everyone know I'm doing this for them, for the American public."

Concern for family members spanned all age brackets. The first letter is from a father to his unborn child. The next two are to a father and grandfather reflecting on the war.

"Dear Katherine Elizabeth

"I wanted to wish you a happy birthday and let you in on a little secret. You are one of the luckiest little girls in the world. You have the most wonderful mother and the greatest big sister any girl could hope for. They both love you very much. They have both made a tremendous effort to bring you into the world. There are no boundaries for their love for you. Please take good care of Mom and Erin.

"Kathy, I wish I could be with you, Erin and Mom today. I hope that someday you will understand why I chose this profession. I want you and your children to live in a peaceful world with all your basic freedoms preserved.

"I will do my best to make up for all our lost time. 'How will I do this?' you might ask. Let me make you a promise. I promise to be your friend; to praise you when you are deserving; to listen when you need to talk; to hug you when you need a hug; to spank you if you need a spanking; and to love you always. I am anxiously awaiting the day when I first hold you in my arms and tell you all of this in person. Love, Dad."

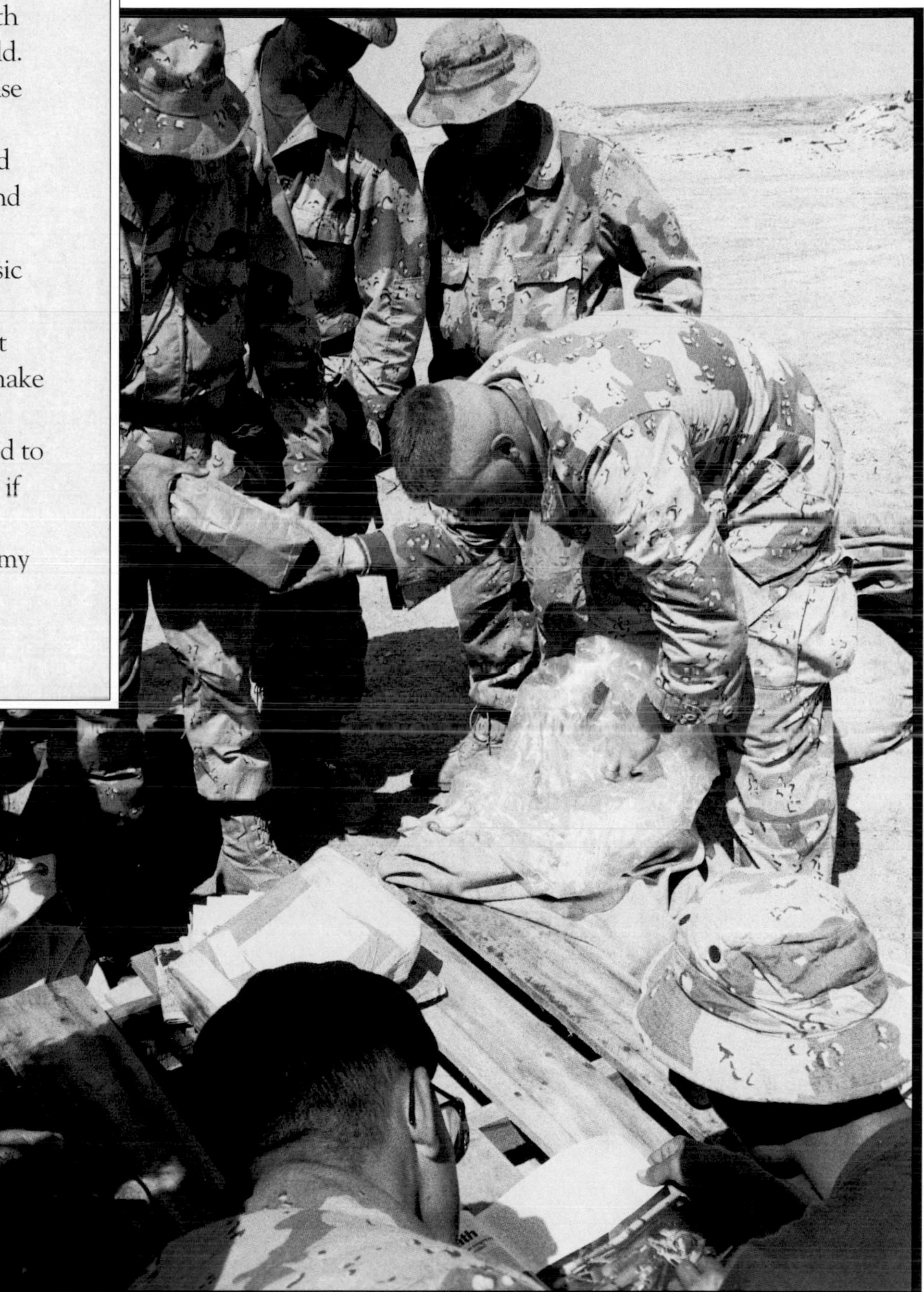

Marine Corps Capt. Dennis Cunniffe addressed this letter to his newborn daughter, Katherine Elizabeth. They finally met when she was seven months old.

Family ties were strengthened when family members went off to war. Marine Sgt. Edgar C. Snyder II, found a new respect for his father, Edgar C. Snyder of Kingwood, WV, after reflecting on his pre-war life.

"Hi, Dad. I got your card today. You had some really excellent advice (as always). The things you mentioned are things that one doesn't always think about day to day. It really is important to strive to be your best and to help others do better any way you can. You taught me well, gave me morals and took time to show me things. I've always believed that any male could be a father but it takes someone special like yourself to be a Dad.

"When I get home we will spend some time together. I've always got time for you. Maybe we can go to a Pirate game. I love you and I'll write you again soon. Thanks for the card and most of all for your prayers."

This letter was written to his grandfather George Willis of Tonawanda, NY, by Lance Cpl. Michael S. Turton. He got a sample of what other wars were like when he asked his grandfather about World War II.

"Dear Grampa. What's up? Thank you for your letter. I didn't know you served under General Patton. Did you ever talk with him? I know how the 81mm gunners are. Those base plates get pretty heavy after awhile, don't they?

"I'd just like to take this time and thank you for all you have done. I've always wanted to tell you thanks for what you did in WW II, but thought it would be too 'mushy,' you know, not mannish. I was quite wrong. I've gotten a taste of what war is like, but you had it much worse than I. I didn't lose any close friends or have to worry about air raids, just chemical warfare and artillery were what I was up against. THANK YOU GRAMPA you are my hero. Take care and God bless! Your Grandson, Mike."

"How are you? We, Melinda and J.C. and me, miss you so much. We love Miss Gabi, Carl and C.J., she takes us everywhere and buys us a lot. But it is not the same as you were here.

"I watch the news on CNN with Miss Gabi every night and I cry and pray you come home soon and safe. J.C. got his first tooth and Melinda is going to the bathroom a little.

"Christmas will be here soon and Miss Gabi is telling us about Santa. My biggest wish is that you both be here for Christmas. I don't want nothing else. Why do people fight and kill each other? That cannot be fun.

"We love you sooo much and miss you and many hugs and kisses from me, Melinda and J.C. I help Miss Gabi a lot."

Miss Lackey adds the following note: "I'm from Germany and I love the United States. The people here are very nice to me and I wanted to do something nice for their country. The parents are home now and have taken charge of the children. I will never forget this experience and, if the situation would occur again I wouldn't hesitate to do it all over again."

When Sgts. Edith and Max Miller were called for duty in Saudi Arabia, they left behind three young children, Jennifer who is 8, Melinda, 2, and J.C., 5 months. They were left in the capable hands of Mr. and Mrs. Carl Lackey. Mr. Lackey is a letter carrier. Mrs. Lackey used to babysit for the family and she took over the children full time. She shares with us this letter Jennifer wrote to her parents.

Bernice Wilson, of Long Beach, CA, was a Navy Nurse in WW II. When she wrote an "any soldier" letter to Operation Desert Storm she got this reply from lst Lt. John. R. Gambrino USMC, a logistics officer.

"Thank you so much for the support message. It is nice to hear from someone with an actual idea of what we go through.

"This has been an extremely long year of deployments for me. By the end of 1990 I will have been separated from my family for eight of the ten months, provided we are here that long. My third wedding annivrsary is 17 October 90 and we have a 15-month old baby.

"Your encouragement helps all of us stay motivated. Keep flying the yellow ribbons and don't forget about us and we will keep our part."

"Dear Dad. I know it is hard for you but you'll be fine. I know you have only been there for a little while but I miss you a lot. Dad when you get back I won't be sucking my thumb any more just for you.

"I know this is a long letter but I am trying to make you happy. It's hard not to think about someone who is far away. I hope you are thinking all about us while you are there. Mom and I can't stop thinking about you and we won't forget you.

"When you left I thought I was going to lose you so don't get hurt. You know, Dad, it's hard to write a letter to someone who is far away. Love Sarah."

Letters from children to their dads overseas often show a developing maturity. Sarah Jean, 9, wrote this letter to her Dad, Tech. Sgt. Robert Shafley. It was the first letter he received in the desert. Her Mom was 7-1/2 months pregnant at the time.

"Until now I wasn't sure how we stood. I never had doubts that it would work out, but I really wasn't sure. Your letter I received today motivated the hell out of me. I have to watch myself because I can't be on Cloud 9 too long. I needed that letter. I need you! Thank you for being there for me. I can't wait to get back to you.

"So, we have a wedding to plan. The guy wouldn't happen to be a 5'10", 150 pounds, blonde hair, blue-eyed jar head would he? You plan. I'm open to whatever you want. I promise to you though that I will never stress again! What do your parents think about having a combat action Marine corporal in the family. Well tell your parents I said hello. If your father writes me I'll write him back. I do not know their address."

This letter was received by Kym Price, Louisville, KY, while her fiance Lance Cpl. Brian P. Willey, USMC, was in Operation Desert Storm.

"My name is Lance Corporal Gary D. Haisman. I am in the Marine Corps and presently deployed on a ship in the Mediterranean Sea.

"My wife, Shannon C. Haisman is currently registered with you at the Family Birth Center. Her due date is May 7. I am scheduled to be deployed until the end of July. I am writing this to let you know this is our first baby. I would like to have the best of everything you have to offer for my wife. She deserves it.

"I unfortunately never got a chance to visit the Center but I hear it is a great place to have a baby. My wife did send some information for me and I was impressed to say the least. I would do anything to be there for her while she's having our baby but my command won't allow it out here.

"I don't know who her doctor is yet but I was wondering if there was any information a proud father should get before hand. Will you please send me anything you can and maybe even monthly check-ups on her?

"I'm trying to get involved thousands of miles away and it's tough. Shannon has been doing a great job though. I am really interested and excited. It's unreal. Will you please take extra-special care of her for me and tell her I care for her and love her."

The second letter is to his mother, Pam Haisman of Fort Myers, FL.

"Dear Mom, I know this isn't much but in case I'm not around: Happy Mothers Day!!

"I think your a perfect Mom. Even though I'm married with my own family now I can always still count on you no matter what and for anything.

"I can always count on that card or letter that gives me the support I need when I am down. You're always there for me even if I think no one else is. I don't tell you this often but you're a great mother and I'm proud to have a Mom like you. I love you Mom, keep up the good work."

This might have been a happy story to tell in this book, but it had a tragic ending. It is told in a series of letters. The first is to Cape Coral Hospital in Florida.

Cpl. Haisman was accidentally shot by another Marine in Iraq on May 3, 1991. He died immediately. His wife of nine months gave birth to his daughter, Alexis, three days later. Gary's grandmother died just one week before he did. His best friend, Stephen, whom they were going to name a boy baby after, died in December 1989. Gary's mother adds this note:

"Gary had a tremendous faith in God and really felt the presence and the peace of those who had gone to heaven before him. He was an extraordinary loving young man who was close to God, close to his family, and longing for the birth of his first child. We are trying hard to keep his loving spirit alive so that his beautiful daughter may grow to know her Daddy."

il Lambert of Andalusia, AL, received this letter from her 19-year-old son Pfc. Wesley Hutts on the day she went to the funeral home to prepare for his burial. He was the first serviceman from Alabama to die in the war. His last letter suggests he may have had a premonition of what was to come. These excerpts are from that letter.

"Mom, I love you and B more than anything in the world. You probably ain't gonna like this letter too much but I feel these things have to be said.

"Let me first tell you why I am over here. Because Kuwait has been invaded by Iraq and we are here to right the wrongs of the world. That's the job of a United States soldier. It is also my job to fight even if we are wrong, which I do not believe that we are. I am fighting here for what I believe is right, the result of the rightness that you and Dad placed in me.

"I am fighting to free an enslaved nation. I am fighting so that Hussein does not use the power that Hitler attained during his Reich.

"Remember the little 6 to 8 year old Saudi girl in Al Sarrar? I am fighting because Hussein is willing to kill her, harm her in any way, and is exposing her to war (a thing she need not be exposed to). He would, if he could, rape, pillage and plunder her household, cause her pain and misery she doesn't deserve, destroy her future. I cannot let that happen and will do all in my power to stop it.

"He would also, if we left him alone, eventually attempt to conquer the states and therefore endangering the two people I love more than anything else, you and B.

"I am fighting because I willingly joined the army to defend democracy against all enemies foreign and domestic. Hussein is an enemy of democracy. I must die for his sins.

"I could tell you about the real reason I must proceed at all costs on my present path, but you will call it male chauvanistic, stupid, worthless or at least a curse or something of that nature. I don't expect you to understand these things the way that I do. Maybe I am living in a dream world, a world that has never, does not and never will exist anywhere but in the hearts, minds and lives of the people who still believe these things are important and self evident as I do.

"I am fighting for my honor, my pride and my ego if you wanna call it an ego. I would not leave even if I could, because if I were to leave under any conditions except death or the end of the war, I could not live with myself. Under no circumstances could I live with myself if I were to leave and betray the soldiers of C Company who placed in my hands possibly their own lives. I could not betray their trust, I love these men too much to do that.

"No matter how much it hurts please accept the way I feel and what I am fighting for and believe in. This is something I must do. It is my destiny, whether one believes in destiny or not, I have seen and accept mine. This letter hurts me more than it hurts you."

"Dear Julia,

"My name is Patrick Legan. I am currently stationed aboard the USS Sacramento which is an auxiliary Oiler and Explosives Ship (AOES). We carry food, fuel, ammunition and office supplies.

"I'd like to say thank you for taking the time to write.

"It has always been my belief that every life has a purpose, some greater and some quieter, but all equally meaningful. Maybe we can't all make important discoveries or create a lasting treasure, but we can accomplish wonderful things with a kind word, a friendly smile, or even a reassuring pat on the back. In fact, in today's difficult world, the person who encourages others is fulfilling one of the finest purposes a life could have.

"Thank you for being that kind of person."

Seaman Patrick Legan, USS Sacramento, received a valentine from Julia Abrantes, New York, NY. His response included his views on the purpose of life.

Spec. Alyssa B. Mehl of the 119th Trans Co., the mother of three small boys, outlined her philosophy of life in this letter to her family in Fort Eustis, VA. It was published as part of a cover story in *USA Today*.

"What have I taught my children? I am a soldier. I am well-trained, confident, honorable and brave. I am part of Operation Desert Shield. My country calls me a hero. I do not cry.

"I am a mother of three small boys. I am half a world away and I cannot comfort them, read bedtime stories, or tell them I love them. My heart breaks. I am still a soldier and I do not cry.

"All of America is watching my performance here and that of my sisters. Our actions may decide women's roles in the armed forces in the future. What will happen to me? Are we going to war against Iraq? Will I be in the midst of battle? What will happen to my children if I die?

"All of our mothers at home want to comfort us. We are so far from home in such uncertain times. My own mother, who usually writes every couple of months, has written me five letters, sent Halloween and Thanksgiving cards and sent care packages. I understand her need to be in touch. I have the same need to be in touch with my children, but they are not grown men trained to kill. They are little boys who should never learn what war is, especially not by losing their mother to one. They need a mother's arms to comfort them, and it breaks my heart to know that I am out of reach, that I made the choice to be a soldier, and that I would do it again. I stole from them a part of their childhood, AND I WOULD DO IT AGAIN.

"I am a soldier, and I do not cry. I am a mother and my heart breaks. If I were to die here for my principles, protecting America's freedoms and interests, I would die wondering what have I taught my children? What have I taken from them?"

"I can't thank you enough for taking the time to write. It amazes me, the support we GIs have back home. People may not agree with the policies that sent us here, but at least they realize we are just soldiers doing our job. I never really thought that I would wind up in something like this. I can tell you right now, there is no other place I would rather be.

"I don't know what the outcome will be over here. I pray that I will make it out alright. But, if I don't, at least I will be able to say I was doing my duty and I was right.

"I am very proud of the guys I am serving with. They are all holding up well and carrying on with the job at hand, under some very trying circumstances. Being somewhat older and having been doing this longer, I do my best to help them through this. I myself have been drawing from that inner reserve you speak of."

Spec. Sean J. Renehan, 24th Inf. Div., responded to a letter from Susan M. Reinteel, Washington, DC. He described himself as "somewhat older" and spoke of pride and devotion to duty.

Army Staff Sgt. Lonnie G. Christensen, son of Mrs. Julaine Christensen, Ray, ND, wrote to thank the community for sending him a package. He included his views on why he was in the Persian Gulf.

"Let me clear up a few things. First off, we would rather be over here now than a few years later down the road. The longer your enemy has a chance to get dug in, the harder it is to dig him out.

"The Iraqis also were working on their ability to develop nuclear weapons. Nukes are not that hard to build any more. And Hussein had most of what he needed.

"Secondly, and I feel strongly, we're all volunteers over here and none of us was drafted. Ten years ago I raised my right hand and swore to uphold and defend my constitution, country's beliefs and interests overseas. I understood that then and still do now. All the people I know feel the same way.

"We are not heroes (no Rambos or John Wayne) we're just a bunch of men and women here to do a job the best we know how and then go home to our loved ones. If America has to be the world's policeman then so be it, someone has to."

"April, Angela and Buford (Girls please read this to Buford. Thank you).

"I love you. This letter is to try to explain to you why I am here and not with you as your friends' fathers are. I love you as much as they love their children. Telling you that I love you is very hard sometimes. The feeling, care and concern for your lives and actions is there. You may not see it, just as I don't seem to understand you and your ways at times. Your Mom always reminds me of that. We are different people each of us with our own thoughts, likes and dislikes.

"I am here because I still feel I owe something to my country. It is probably a debt that I can never pay. But I will try as my country needs me. Our country is one of the richest in freedoms and independence, freedoms that we have earned through many a hardship. Something each of you should never take for granted.

"We are a caring people who help others that respect the same things we do. The country of Kuwait is one of those that share and hold the same principles as we do."

First Sgt. B. R. Kenton, Hq. 7th Grp. (Provost S-2), used these words to explain to his children why he had to be overseas.

"Life here is not all that pleasant but it is bearable so I will not complain too much.

"The hardest part is not being around my friends. I have been assigned as the officer in charge of a new task force. I have all new people working for me and none of my friends are near.

"The primary mission is to clear minefields and break thru antitank obstacles so that the follow on forces can attack. My unit is composed of tanks (armored personnel carriers) and combat engineers.

"It is a position with lots of responsibility. But it also has drawbacks. I have not told this to my Marines but I would like to tell you...my unit is expected to have a 50% casualty rate. The higher ups even consider that to be acceptable. I have only told my Marines that our mission is very important to the success of the ground invasion of Kuwait.

"My outlook has been fluctuating from positive to negative but I think I finally have control over it and I have decided that it will do me no good to worry.

"I am more afraid for my Marines than I am for me. I don't want anything to happen to them but chances are something will."

This letter from Marine Lt. Stephen Herrera was received by Lisa Sorber of Hunlock Creek, PA. It reflects the deep concern officers felt for the welfare of the men under their command.

"I have great disrespect to those servicemen and women who fail to fulfill their obligations to serve our country as they swore they would and then hide behind the term 'conscientious objector.' They too, I am sure, joined the service for career development with hopes to achieve their goals. Yet, when our country calls upon them to do their jobs in time of trouble, they turn their backs on the United States of America and their fellow comrades in arms.

"Prior to leaving the US for the Gulf, I read a passage which I hold in high regard. The name of the person who wrote it fails me, but it reads as follows:"

"War is an ugly thing, but not the ugliest of things, the decayed and the degraded state of moral and patriotic feelings which think that nothing is worth fighting for is much worse. A man who has nothing for which he is willing to fight, nothing he cares about more than his own personal safety is a miserable creature who has no chance of being free unless made and kept so by the exertions of better men than himself."

Warrant Officer David G. Plasch, US Army, seemed to have a premonition of danger when he wrote this letter to his sister, Lynn in Bayside, NY.

On February 27, 1991, while carrying out a mission, David's UH-60 Blackhawk was shot down by enemy fire. Lynn says, "He is dearly missed and never out of our thoughts or our hearts."

Bob Clarke, a sailor aboard the USS Theodore Roosevelt, sent this letter to his father Robert Clarke of Winthrop, MA. In it he compares the Gulf War to his childhood games — only this time, the bullets and the blood were real.

"A solemn thoughtfulness has fallen over me. I am calm, I do not yet fear the unknown. I walk proudly towards whatever tomorrow may bring me. I think back to the carefree days of my early childhood when war was a game played with friends in your own backyard.

"The guns were make believe and so was death. I can remember many arguments where I just knew that I had 'killed' the enemy (my friend Richie) before he 'killed' me. Imagination was our battlefield and, when the peace flag was raised, off we went to our homes, visions of dinner swimming teasingly through our heads. Life was just a game. Not so now, no more make believe.

"Tonight, soldiers clean their weapons in preparation for battle. Aircraft loaded down with bombs are checked thoroughly before flight. Ships race to get into position to support amphibious units. But what of the men? Without the men and women who wear the various uniforms of our armed services, these machines are but pieces of lifeless metal. These are the finest men in the world, and I am fiercely proud to be associated with them."

Being away from home at Christmastime is a painful experience. It becomes even more acute when you are in a war zone thousands of miles from your loved ones. First Lt. Roger Kern spent such a Christmas in Saudi Arabia. His pain was eased a bit by the receipt of a package from the people at St. Mary's Church in Avoca, IA. He and his wife were married in the church in 1984.

"Thank you so much for the care package. There is no way to describe the feeling of getting mail over here. Often receiving the mail is only a small part of the joy. The big payoff is knowing people are thinking about you.

"As you can imagine, church services over here are different and far between. There are not enough priests and training often precludes planned services. I did have the chance to make it to Christmas Mass but it was an all-religions service. One thing that struck me funny was when the part of the shepherds watching over the flocks was brought up. In the past I had always pictured a grassy field, a dog and maybe some trees. Believe me the shepherds over here look dirty, have turbans, sick-looking sheep and, as far as you can see, nothing green. The dog may be an option, but grass is out and sand is in."

"It's Christmas Eve and although I am sharing a tent with eleven other men I feel as lonely as I can ever remember feeling. This is the night when time stands still. I recall a night when I gave you a wedding ring and made beautiful, quiet love while thinking about an entire life to share together. Time stood still for a few moments then.

"When you're a kid it takes forever for Christmas Day to come. You don't get any sleep and you keep waiting for a beam of light to come creeping through the window.

"...Just when I thought that Christmas Eve was safe for sleeping and passing the hours of darkness with a toss and a turn and a few pleasant dreams, I am cast into another time warp created by the uncontrollable desire to hold you and kiss you and make soft quiet beautiful love to you while thinking about an entire life time to share together.

"I love you, Babe. What more can I say. You are my Christmas, my life, my everything."

Tech. Sgt. Donald E. Stephens found himself very lonely on Christmas Eve. In his loneliness he found comfort in a touching love letter to his wife Debbie in Tacoma, WA.

"Just a short letter to say Hi. I love you and I miss you. All is well here and I am doing guard duty later tonight. Maybe I will see Santa and his sleigh! I hope our air defense doesn't shoot him down.

"The following poem or whatever you want to call it is basically just some thoughts I had in my head. It comes from my heart and I mean every word, especially, the very last part. I want to thank you for all you have done for me."

Spec. James P. Raynoha, 82nd Airborne Division, sent this letter and poem to his parents, Martha and Charles Raynoha of Babylon, NY, on Christmas Eve.

"You gave me life and raised me,
from a boy to a man.
You taught me wrong from right
You showed me life and said;
'Do the best you can.'

"Well here it is years later,
An airborne soldier is what I am
To make you proud is all I wanted
and I hope right now you are.

"For now I stand in Desert Sand
I hold my weapon tight in hand,
and stare into the night.
But as I look my thoughts stray
Away, of home and friends and you.

"There is one thing I want to say it is,
You're thought of every day!

"Sometimes I wish that I could be
that boy again.
For when I was scared you protected me;
through thick and through thin.

"But now I am a man, with my
country to defend
I am not afraid, nor shaken or
have any fear of death.
This is my job, I chose to do it
and I truly have no regret.

"But as I stand here in the night
There's just one thing I wish I knew
And that is if you can hear me say;

"Mom and Dad I LOVE YOU!"

Training continues even when units are in the combat zone. Patty Opstad of Waynesboro, VA, received a description of a training exercise from her nephew, HM2 Don Murray who was with the Marines on the USS Denver.

"Since I wrote to you last we did a training exercise in the country of Oman. Man, talk about desolate, nothing but sand, rocks and coral reef, and, oh Yea, camels! A whole lot of wild camels. Apparently the part of the country we were doing our exercise in was covered by water at some point in time, that's why there's so much sand and coral reef.

"Humping, that's the Marine word for marching, through the desert with a 50-60 pound pack is really not my idea of a good time. It's even harder when you go through sand, your feet are always sinking and it doesn't seem like you're going anywhere. Our first day we kept shaded from the sun. It gets awful hot at night.

"We moved about 6 miles to some rock formation the commanders set up as an enemy position. Needless to say, we killed all the rocks, took no prisoners and suffered no casualties. Pretty good for our first conflict with unarmed rocks. I hope the Iraqi's fight the same way."

COMMANDANT
ARIZONA
BRAND

Sr. M. Sgt. Ronald G. Belknap of the Air National Guard Unit at Rickenbacker, ANGB, OH, tried to ease his loneliness by focusing on the needs of his troops. In this letter to his wife Cynthia in Westerville, OH, he tells how he helped himself by helping others.

"I have been in this country for forty five days. In that time I have seen and delicately handled many things. Some have been fantastic and some have been sad. I have been away from my family on Christmas Eve and Christmas Day. I finished 1990 without family however, I was here with the best of friends.

"I was here when the war started. I have seen men demoted. I have seen men promoted. I have been with men on their last day of service and also been in the room where men raised their right hand to reenlist in the service.

"I have tried to console men that just received a Dear John letter or a letter from their wife asking for a divorce. But, I also have shared the happiness of a man calling his girlfriend and asking her to marry him and they say yes. I have seen a man die of a heart attack, and a fellow soldier receive word that he's a father.

"I have seen white men and black men come together and work as one. I have seen men and women coming from all different backgrounds from all over the United States work together for one goal. I have seen more patriotism than I can ever tell you. I am proud of my men and we are proud to be here and will do our best for our country."

Many of the troops realized they were making history in the Gulf. This gave them "bragging rights" when they wrote to the folks back home. Mrs. Mary Taylor of Benton, IL, shared this letter from Air Force Maj. Richard Tennant Jr., of the 492nd Tactical Fighter Squadron.

"It may interest you to know that our wing is the only U.S. Air Force Fighter Wing to have an official name — 'The Statue of Liberty Wing.' The wing acquired the name after the second world war when it was stationed in France and the local French people presented the wing with a miniature statue of liberty.

"I'm with the 492nd Tactical Fighter Squadron. Our nickname is 'The Mad Hatters.' This was again acquired in France when the squadron members wore French berets. The squadron now wears the 'English Bowler' hat on special occasions.

"I flew a mission the first night of the war against an Iraqi air field. I was also on a sortie at night against Iraqi tanks in Southeast Iraq the night the ground war started. And, I flew a sortie the last night of the war near the Iraqi city of Al Barah. So it was unique in a way to be flying at the start and end of the war."

BMI (SW) Cecil Garrett, of the Navy's SAM Detachment, tells his parents, Mr. and Mrs. Richard Raymond, Cynthiana, KY, how the ship on which he was serving became the first US Navy vessel to land in Kuwait.

"Well, I guess you can say I made history about four days ago. After we finished running our minesweep patterns around the mouth of the harbor we had a loss of communications with SAM so I took two other guys and our rubber rafts and went to get it. SAM had drifted only about 100 yards from land when we got to it. I got on board with another 1st class and we drove it manually up on the beach and tied it to a pier at the mouth of the harbor.

"I got off of SAM and was standing on the pier smoking a cigaret and an Army captain who works with the ground forces in Kuwait came up and was talking to us. He said that technically that was the first U.S. Navy vessel to land in Kuwait since the war started August 2.

"We pulled our tug into the harbor three days ago and since then the USS Lasalle has pulled into where we had already cleared it out. They had a two-star admiral on board when they pulled in and they had a band and CNN to cover it and make a big press deal of it. But I can always say I know whose feet touched first because those feet were in my shoes. Just something to tell Matthew when he is old enough to understand."

Mrs. Ruth Murray of Silverstrand, CA, is very proud of her daughter Joette who was promoted to sergeant in Iraq. Joette is one of a team of three female linguists who call themselves "The Dream Team." During their seven plus months in Saudi Arabia their language skills made them in great demand in the forward areas. Their mission made them the most northern (closest to the front) females in the conflict. She said they were so far forward they didn't even know Bob Hope was visiting the troops. This excerpt is from one of Joette's letters.

"Julie just left to pick up the mail and everyone knows it. It's funny, they all watch her take off in Bertha (our truck) every night at around 6 or 7. She comes back down the hill beeping her horn screaming 'Mail Call' and soon all of Team Dragon is surrounding her hoping to hear their names.

"Mom, don't worry. I'll never quit. You've been the perfect role model for me as well as my best friend. I'll never quit because someday I want a child who likes, loves and respects me as much as I do you. It must be a nice feeling Mom to be your own kid's hero."

"I think they should pass a special law that people who are in the service, especially ones who were over here, can legally drink. I'll be so — off to come home and not be old enough to buy beer. I guess there are a lot more things to worry about, but it's an idea anyway.

"At least I can vote now. Lot of good that does me in 1991. The next elections aren't til '92, right?"

Pvt. Cody Frasure of the lst Cavalry Division may be America's youngest soldier serving in Operation Desert Storm. He celebrated his 18th birthday in Iraq. In his letter he wonders if he still will be an "adult" when he returns to the United States.

Capt. Susan Clarke wrote this letter from Saudi Arabia to her parents, Mr. and Mrs. Audrey H. Clarke in Duluth, MN. She was the last flight nurse coming back from her unit the 109th Aeromed Evac.

"I have something exciting to tell you. I went out on a C-130 mission on March 1 up to the front line (eight miles from the Kuwait border) and had the honor of bringing back the <u>last</u> of our wounded soldiers. Those guys looked so exhausted - I had 13 ambulatory patients - the rest were on litters, and I got to talk to each one of them.

"They looked so tired - some talked, some smiled, some were in pain. Some just looked straight ahead but you know what - they all looked so <u>proud</u>.

"Each time I write this I get tears in my eyes. As long as I live I'll never forget their eyes. I finally got a chance to do what I came over here to do. I'm happy. I'm happy it's over, I'm glad our casualties were so low and I am happy the guys can go home now! Isn't it great!

"The wounds were mostly shrapnel type - few burns and few dislocations. One guy's cheeks were wrapped. An AK-47 went in and out of his cheeks. Another had burns on his face and both hands wrapped - he's a tank driver. He was looking out the top hole of the tank as they were blowing up an Iraqi tank when there was a flash explosion and he got burned. His buddy on top of the tank was killed.

"One kid on a litter with both feet wrapped stepped on a land mine. Broken bones and open fractures.

"When we landed and unloaded them they went on a helo right over to the Army hospital. Every one at the MASH tent was falling all over us. They all wanted to help get those guys taken care of!

"It was great when we watched the litter loaders move the guys on the litters pass us. The patients looked up, gave a thumbs up and mouthed thanks. I'll never forget this."

Civilians, often children, suffer greatly in war, even though they are innocent victims caught in the clash of combatants. Steve Eureste shares his pity for the children in this letter to his wife Shelly. Both are now stationed with the 12th Evacuation Med Hospital.

"It's been in the last week that I had to see the terrible side of war that nobody ever talks about and now I know the reason. The hospital has been crowded with Iraqi civilian casualties, mostly women and children caught in between firefights between Republican Guard and rebels.

"I've been helping a lot in the operating room although it is very hard concentrating on work when there's a four-year-old lying on the table with multiple gunshot or scrap metal injuries.

"I helped with this nine-year-old girl that was hit with scrap metal from a land mine. It took off part of her frontal portion of the skull and severed her eye. We reconstructed her entire front skull with wire. It looked like a puzzle. We had to take out her eye but she'll live. I felt so sorry for her I gave her that little bear you sent for Valentine's Day. She smiled and said thank you in Arabic.

"I almost lost my composure a couple of days ago. I helped take this little boy to the intensive care unit after surgery. Earlier that morning we had to amputate his leg. He stepped on a land mine. This old man stood crying and walked away from his little boy.

"I took him aside and told him everything was going to be all right. Shelley, he looked just like a street person. I had to fight my tears back. I later found out that he had lost his wife and four other kids.

"I'm really depressed when I leave the operating room and keep thinking about what or where these people are going from here. I can at least go home but these people can't. The Saudis don't want anything to do with them and look down on the Army for bringing them into their country.

"The Iraqis are trickling in slowly and I just take one day at a time and deal with as it happens. I love you and I am sorry if this letter sucks, but that's what is happening."

"You wouldn't believe it up here Mom. Thousands of tents housing the Kurds are up in the mountains of Turkey. I've never seen anything like it before. It was total craziness when we were dropping off food and supplies. I mean chaos. We would drop it off and these Kurds would be hanging on the helicopter after we picked up 10 feet in the air. It's settled down a lot now flying them back into the city. The only bad part is that they don't smell too good. Oh well.

"Well, I am enclosing a 'Saddam Bill.' I bought it from a 'Hey Joe' outside the gate in Zachu. I just couldn't force myself to buy a turban so I got you this. Hold it up to the light and you'll be able to see his face on the other side."

This letter from Cpl. R. A. Hort, 24th MEV Det. 7, to his mother, Ms. Jean Hort of Upper Marlboro, MD, tells of the desperate plight of civilians in the war zone.

Some American troops had an opportunity to dine with Arab families. How they reacted to Arab food — and to field food in general — is noted in these excerpts from some of their letters home.

"I have no desire for a medal or a Purple Heart. I'd much rather see myself and my men come home alive and well.

"Please let any anti-war protestors back home know that there is nothing more demoralizing to a 19-year-old Marine who is about to lay his life on the line for his friends and country than to listen to a bunch of whining, ignorant people complain of him being here and what he is doing.

"I know their intentions are good. But, they should shut up and let us get this thing over with."

Mrs. Lenore Smith of Princeton, NJ, shares a letter from her son, Lt. Mike Ragoza who served in the Marines during Desert Storm. She says his experience was unique in that, out of the 500,000 troops, he wound up being interviewed on CNN and was quoted nationally in the press. This happened because it was his platoon that led the first ground battle at Khafji. He was awarded a Bronze Star for valor for his courage and leadership at Khafji and Kuwait.

The foods enjoyed by the Arabs were as much a mystery to the U.S. troops as the Arab customs and way of life. Sgt. Chris J. O'Donnell, Hq. RLT-4, tells what happened when he was "the man who came to dinner." Parts of his letter were published in his hometown newspaper in Winchester, IL.

"During the month of November I had the opportunity to meet with some Saudi Arabian Marines. In doing so I learned a lot about Arab customs and way of life. What I found most interesting was the way that they conduct a meal. This is the way we had dinner with the Saudis.

"While the food was being prepared we all sat on the Persian carpeted floor and drank small glasses of bitter Saudi Arabian coffee. After coffee, very sweet tea was served and we talked amongst ourselves until it was time to eat.

"Dinner was served; the cooks carried in huge platters the size of a saucer sled. On them was piles of rice topped with a whole freshly roasted lamb. When I say whole I mean whole! That means head and tail included. These platters were set on the floor and about eight people circled each one sitting on one knee.

"When the word was given to commence, each person leaned toward the food and took a handful of rice or lamb or both. The object was to pack the rice together with your hand and pop it into your mouth. Talk about messy! dropped more on the carpet than I ended up eating. The beverage served was none other than Pepsi. After eating it was off to the bathroom to wash up. My afterthoughts were that I felt like a member of a caveman tribe feeding on the kill of the day."

2nd Lt. Robin Richey of the lst Medical Group, 41st Combat Support Hospital, tells her best friend, Holly A. Greer of San Antonio, TX, about the special problems confronting a woman when dining with a Saudi family.

"A few weeks ago I had an opportunity to go with my boss (the LTC) to dinner at a Saudi's house. The guy owns the land our hospital is on. So he took me to this place - wow! The men all wore robes and head dresses. The house has several very empty rooms. They just have cushions along the walls to sit on.

"The women never mix with the men. In fact, they live in a separate house. I was fortunate being a female to be allowed to go. They are trying to accept our culture.

"Anyway, I ate with these people - all men - on the floor with my hands. They do not use forks or spoons. Have you ever tried to eat rice with your hands?

"I was able to go to the ladies house and visit too. None of the men went. They wear veils over their faces. We had an interpreter for the men and the ladies had some girls who spoke a little English. It was a fantastic experience. I was there for about six hours. It was great."

Spec. Larry Chambers of the lst Cavalry Division had at least one memorable meal in Operation Desert Storm. He was one of 70 soldiers invited to eat with visiting General Colin Powell. He describes the encounter in this letter to Laura Bronski, Staten Island, NY.

"Well, today, we had the visit of Gen Colin Powell to the compound where we are. Myself and nine others from our company went to have dinner with him (among some 70 other troops).

"You would probably expect a big fancy dinner due to the visit of such a military figure. Well, guess what? We had some T rations (Lasagna) which by the way it was good. He ate and then signed some autographs.

"He said the President and the American people are 100% behind us and that he can relate to what we are going through. He also said we should be praying that the crisis resolves peacefully. But, if worse comes to worse, we should be ready for combat to go and do our job with the least possible number of victims It was pretty good, not that I was impressed, but...."

Sgt. Donald A. Norman served in Bahrain. After three weeks of eating MREs he decided his family should have first hand knowledge of combat cuisine. He sent his parents, Mr. and Mrs. Marvin Norman of Greensboro, NC, what he called a "care package." This is the letter that accompanied the package.

"Hello and how are you today? Hungry I hope. Real hungry! Now that you obviously have opened the box up, let's take a few moments to ponder its contents. We have one vial of genuine sand, one bottle of hot sauce, one American flag, and not one but two delectable MRE dinners. Additional items needed for your meal but unable to ship include: water at room temperature, scorching sunlight, sharp knife and, lastly, an operational toilet or the equivalent thereof.

"Now that you have all of the above items, we are ready to enjoy our dinner. First, take the vial of sand and dump half of it out on the ground (for seating purposes only. The rest will be used later). Have a large glass of tent temperature (95 degrees) water beside you and open your MRE with your sharp knife. The reason for the sharp knife is I can't guarantee your meal is dead yet so open with caution. Dump out its contents. Doesn't it look yummy?

"Under no circumstances are you to heat this up or spice it up with anything other than what was given you in the package. As you eat, periodically throw some of the remaining sand on your food and face for full effect. After eating try the delicious coffee with cold water.

"Even if you don't drink it, try to dissolve the coffee creamer and sugar in cold water just for fun. Enjoy your coffee for about 10 or 15 minutes then stand by with your American flag in your right hand. Shortly thereafter you will need to take your flag and run like hell to the nearest operational toilet. The waving of the flag symbolizes you have eaten an American government MRE and survived.

"I hope you enjoyed this small taste of what we are eating at night here in the land of nothing but sand. It's the closest I could bring you to what we are living like (only on certain occasions, like starvation).

"Take care and Pepto Bismol."

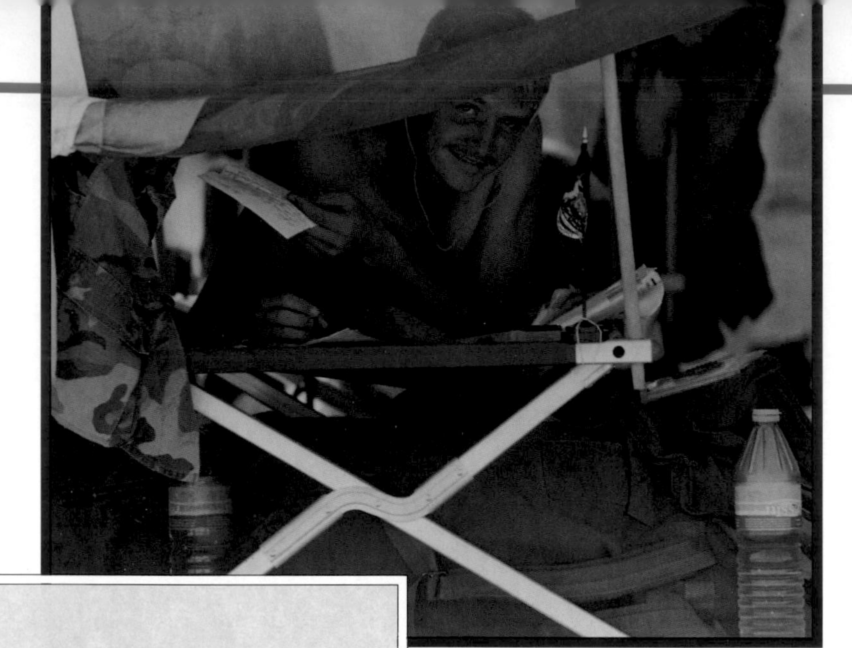

Even the quality of the food was forgotten when it was time for mail call. Some of the soldiers were so happy to get mail they wrote "thank-you" letters to their letter carriers.

"Well I'm here in the middle of the biggest bunch of nowhere I've ever been.

"Tents as far as the eye can see and sand enough to keep every kid in the U.S. covered up to his neck.

"If you guys can think of anything to send over to make life better, send it. Anything will be well received. Ask John to send me an owl feather if he can. I lost the one I found in Louisiana in a windstorm. I have become noted over the base as the feathered hat man."

"The food is OK. We get two hot meals, breakfast and dinner. Lunch and midnight meals are MREs (meals ready to eat) dehydrated. Most of them taste like a camel spit in them."

Mr. and Mrs. Cliff Cody of Union, OH, had two sons, Mike and Terry, serving in Operation Desert Storm. Tech. Sgt. Mike of the 23rd IFW/SMS Deployed had these observations about the food he was getting.

"Mail is an uplifter of the spirits. It can change your entire day. The public's support means the most.

"It gives us motivation and faith. It is hard to be so far away from our homes and loved ones. The words of encouragement from people such as all of you make it easier."

This letter was written to Mrs. Gerald Riggs and the ladies of the Meherrian Baptist Church in Murfreesboro, NC, by her grandson U.S. Army Sgt. Gregory B. Harris while he was serving in Saudi Arabia with the 82nd Airborne Division.

"As an Air Force pilot who saw combat in Southeast Asia as well as the Persian Gulf, I can assure you it gives me a warm feeling to see this happening across America.

"Many wounds from Vietnam are being healed in the Persian Gulf. A quote I heard the other day went like this: 'Ghosts from Vietnam are being buried in the sands of Arabia.'

"Believe me, those of us here have noticed the support and backing of the American people at home. I see America writing in a way that hasn't happened in a long time. I see more people in church and praying for our troops overseas. I see people standing up to the counter, taking pride in our nation and simply saying 'I am an American and proud of it'."

Mayor Pete Heine of Baker, LA, wrote letters to men and women from his town serving in Operation Desert Storm. Among the answers he got was this letter from Maj. Wayne Wroten.

"Sorry I don't have a Christmas card to send you but I'll take this opportunity to wish you all the happiest of holidays.

"As usual, the holidays represent a real increase in work for you guys, especially now with so many thousands away from home, so I just want to thank you personally for all you've done and are still doing for us.

"Wars may be fought with aircraft and bullets, but one seldom acknowledged piece of critical ammunition we have is provided by you - word from back home. Thanks for doing your part too - every man and woman over here needs that support!

"Take care. God Bless and keep up the good work! If nobody else takes the time to thank you enough, I hope my sincere feelings help make up for it."

USAF Lt. Steve Parker was so happy to get his mail that he wrote a "thank-you" letter to his Postmaster in Millville, MA.

"Just want to let you know that I am fine. You guys at the post office must be doing a great job because the mail keeps coming. Yesterday I heard that we have three large airplanes bringing mail over each day packed with packages, cards and letters.

"Each day here has its moments with the scud missile launches. Every day those missile launchers send us scrambling to put on our gas masks and chemical ensembles (overcoats, pants and boots). So far they haven't hit us. I love those Patriot missiles. God is watching over me."

Postal employees can take great satisfaction from the letters they have received thanking them for a job well done. Terry M. Galvan, a Mail Handler, in Santa Ana, CA, shares this letter from her brother, Air Force Capt. Arthur M. Galvan of the 16th SOS.

"I can tell you that receiving the mail was the absolute highlight of any day. Though I was able to telephone my family now and then, the letters, cards, pictures and packages meant the most to me. At one point an entire elementary school in Apollo Beach, Florida, sent me a box of 1,000 handmade Christmas decorations which I distributed to hundreds of troops during my travels to various units throughout the theater. Many thanks to the members of the U.S. Postal Service for making our holidays bright and bringing us a small part of 'home' during the war.

"More that any other factor, the tons of mail we received created an unbreakable link between the American public and the U.S. fighting forces. It was as if your families, friends and neighbors were there with us, sharing our experiences, feeling our pain, and lifting our spirits."

Maj. Richard M. Chapin wrote the Postal Service about the importance of mail to the troops. He wrote after his return home from the Persian Gulf.

As important as mail was to the troops, it had to compete with other priorities for delivery to the field. Lt. Col. B. H. Borum, 24th Inf. Div., in this letter to Mrs. Meiree Arnold, Marion, IA, explained the priority system.

"I think that I have received all of the packages you sent me during my deployment in the Middle East. However I am afraid that many of the packages mailed to me as well as to countless other GIs will never arrive.

"Combat operations sometimes result in the less than absolute priorities being disregarded. In Iraq the U.S. maintained the following priorities (1) fuel, (2) ammunition, (3) repair parts, (4) water, (5) food, (6) medical supplies and (7) other.

"Mail, although given a very high priority, was still part of the 'other' category. However, before we would let undeliverable care packages go to waste, we would give them to "any GI." Privates got the packages that obviously contained treasures; cookies, dried fruits, candy, Kool Aid, etc. Lieutenant colonels got the 'any soldier' letters from nursing homes. I answered every one of the nursing home letters.

"I was one of the last members of my brigade to leave Saudi Arabia. I commanded the Stay Behind detachment which provided the final equipment preparation for shipment actions. It was not until I boarded the PanAm plane for the return trip that my troops and I realized how much support our fellow countrymen had provided us.

"There were no radio stations in the desert. While in Saudi Arabia and Iraq I thought that most Americans understood the importance of what we were doing, the vocal minority would be the only voices addressing the war. I must admit that our learning just how much we had been supported by America was a very humbling experience."

Jane and Rolf Kruger flank Rogelio and Mrs McLean during a reunion at the McLean home.

"Hi Bud. Hoping this letter finds you and your family in the best of health and good spirits.

"You are just about the best above the best. Thanks a million for contacting my loved ones. I'll bow to anyone who looks out for my family my good amigo.

"I've been married going on 23 years. I know my wife from when we were very young. She is a tremendous lady, which I'll never trade for another. I've got five more years to retire, 20 years is enough for me. I plan to retire in Panama and do as you said, fish, exercise, travel and take it real easy."

This letter from Mrs. Rolf Kruger, East Greenwich, RI, shares a response her family got to her "any soldier" letter to the Gulf and how the families rejoiced together when the war was over.

"After the first letter from Sgt. McLean my husband took over. He was interested that Sgt. McLean was from Panama because my husband speaks, reads and writes Spanish.

"We called his wife on the phone several times and established a pleasant relationship. When Sgt. McLean returned home to Fort Dix he phoned us and we joined his family there in a welcome home celebration.

"The enclosed picture shows the four of us at the McLean home. We hope they will come to New England in the not too distant future so we can extend as warm hospitality to them as they did to us."

2nd Lt. Michael Phillips of the First Cavalry Division used a poem to express his thanks to Rachel Evans, age 9, a third grader from Arlington, TX, who sent a valentine to the Persian Gulf soldiers.

"Hello to great 3rd graders from the U.S.A.,
From a soldier, so far away.

"I read all your poems, not once, but twice,
I loved them all. They were so very nice.

"I'd tell you this in person, if I were there,
It feels so good to know you all care.

"How was your Christmas? Was he good to you?
Believe it or not, he came here too.

"Feel free to write again. I'll keep in touch,
Again, thanks for your poems. Thank you very much!"

Aviation Storekeeper First Class Daniel Feliciano serving in the Persian Gulf on the aircraft carrier John F. Kennedy received an illustrated letter from his seven-year-old niece, Danielle Gutierrez of Del Valle, TX.

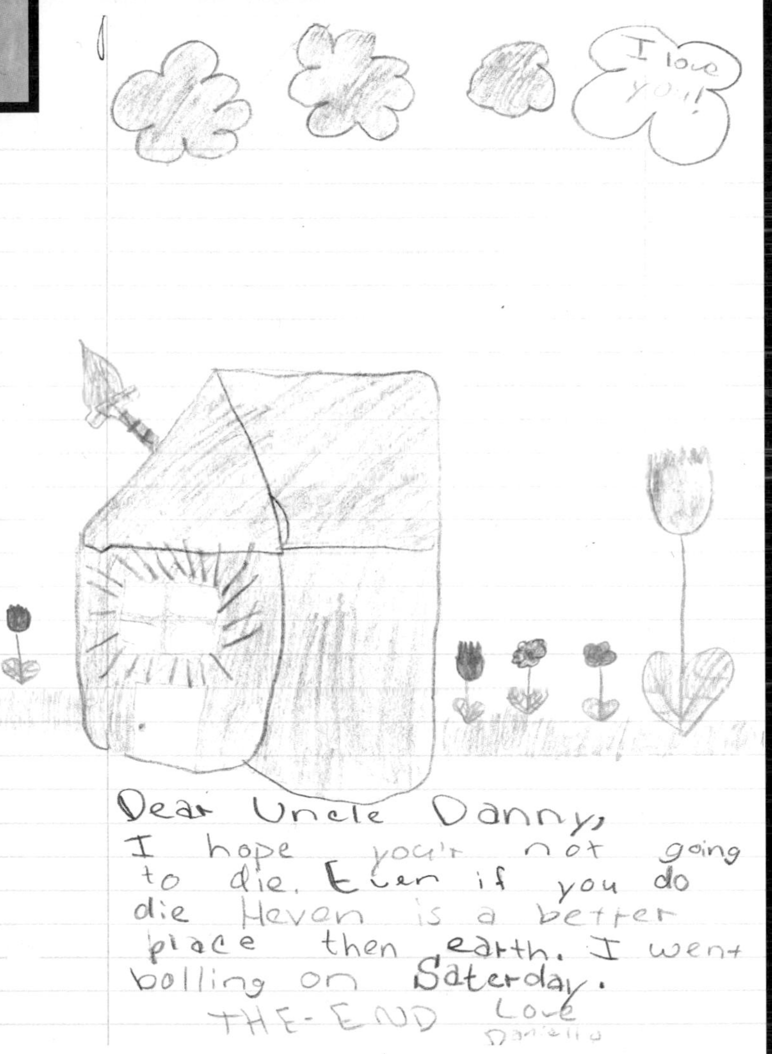

I love you!

Dear Uncle Danny,
I hope you'r not going to die. Even if you do die Heven is a better place then earth. I went bolling on Saterday.
THE-END Love
Danielle

In January 1991 Maxine Coufal, Postmaster, Cotesfield, NE, saw an article in the newspaper asking people to send nylons to any service member. She sent a package of them and received a response from lst Lt. J. Meskill of the lst Infantry Division.

"I passed the nylons on to our battalion maintenance officer. He's come up with some innovative uses for them. They work great covering the air intake vent on the Highly Mobile Multi-purpose Wheeled Vehicle (HMMWV). We gave one pair to the assistant division chaplain for his HMMWV. I also put a pair over the filter of our TACCS computer which we use for processing personnel related business.

"They also work great for covering rifles and pistols. Who would have guessed that panty hose would have so many uses in keeping sand out of equipment?"

"The weather here has turned to fall/winter for this part of the world so the temperatures are a lot more bearable than when we arrived. Despite the drop in the temperature, we are still required to drink 5-6 bottles of water per day, but nowhere near the 5-6 gallons that was mentioned on the news. We have not had any problems with the local 'critters,' though everyone has seen more than their share of snakes, scorpions and especially camels."

Once a rule is made it is very difficult to get it changed, even though the original conditions have changed. One example can be found in this excerpt from a letter to Ray and Julie Newnam of Brier, WA, from Staff Sgt. Timothy G. Fredrikson.

Most military people assigned to the Persian Gulf had very little chance to get close to an Arab woman. When they did, the encounter was brief and uneventful. An exception was described by Pfc. Rick Mroos in his letter to the Richardson family of Seattle, WA.

"Our truck stopped in an area where four or five little kids were playing. They ran up to me babbling raghead at me. I did what soldiers have done with kids for hundreds of years. I broke out my food and shared it with them. For some reason the kids all over the world like Army food while we cant stand it.

"While I'm messing with these kids I hear female voices coming from the doorway. This arab girl comes out to get the kids and I guess she sees me. Whenever arab women go out in public they have to wear those bedsheet things around them. Well I guess since she had been in the house she didn't have one on. This girl was beautiful. She was wearing an outfit like something out of 'I Dream of Jeannie' but I could still tell she had a knockout body.

"She says something to the kids. I think she was telling them to go inside. The kids started crying and complaining so she let them stay. She points at my helmet which is on the ground and I hand it to her. She pulls out a picture I had inside. It was of me when I was at a camp in Southern Saudi Arabia. She says something I didn't understand. So, me being a wise guy, I shake my head yes and say 'Alright.' She puts the picture in her pocket.

"She points to the patch on my shoulder. I didn't know how to say I was a paratrooper so I drew a picture of a guy in a parachute and pointed at myself. She nodded her head and said about the same thing she said when she asked for my picture. So I ripped off my patch and gave it to her. I'm thinking damn next she will want my boots. But, she gave me this bracelet she was wearing. It was white ivory with blue arab writing of some prayer out of their bible or whatever they call it.

"Then, I heard this high pitched scream and this dumpy old arab woman comes storming out of the house with a broom in her hand. Her and the girl started arguing and the old lady points inside the house. Then, wham, the old bag knocked me upside the head with the broom. About that time my sergeant yells for me to get back on the truck so I split.

"As we were pulling out the girl yells out the window and waves to me. So every night she probably gazes at my picture and thinks what could have been. It ain't easy flirting when you don't know the language."

"...When the POWs got back to the ship and were being interrogated one of them said, 'Do you know what you are doing to my country?' The interrogator replied 'Yes we do. Do you know what you did to Kuwait?' All the interrogator got was a sullen look.

"The Iraqis hadn't eaten in quite a while. Oddly enough they had lots and lots of rice on their island, they had no water to cook it in. Dry rice is not easy to eat. After the medical examination they were fed the same dinner we had that night, Steak and King Crab. No kidding, that really was the dinner that night. The Iraqis had never seen King Crab, they weren't excited about it. They ate the steak like it was their first real food in a long time—it was.

"Between mouthfuls of steak, potato, corn, cherry cobbler and ice cream, one of them said: 'If our fellow soldiers knew you would serve them food like this they would swim to your ship to surrender.' Maybe we should have dropped food instead of bombs."

In this letter to his aunt, Mrs. Renie Peterson of Bellingham, WA, Cmdr. Richard Sluys tells how Iraqis reacted when they were taken prisoner.

Allied soldiers who took prisoners frequently found themselves pitying their captives. Spec. Shane Sorensen of the 317th Engr. Bn. wrote his mother, Sheila Sorensen, Great Falls, MT, about his experience in dealing with POWs.

"I had to guard some guys that surrendered today. Really I was assigned to just one later. But something happened that kinda upset me. The guy I was guarding was the first to be questioned. (There were four of them, one was a colonel). I had to reach down and help him up from where he was sitting. My hand almost went around his entire arm.

"Then, as we were walking from his group, he turned and asked me something in Arabic. I have never ever seen such fear in a man's eyes.

"The interpreter walking beside him told me when I started to ask him what he said, that he was asking if I was going to kill him. He thought I was leading him to an execution. I just wished I spoke Arabic so I could tell him what was going on.

"When I realized what he had said it was like someone took my breath away. It might not sound like much to you, but it is a terrible feeling to have someone look at you like that. It bothered me all day.

"Turns out he is 22 and was drafted into the military three months ago. As soon as he and his buddy read pamphlets (from bombers) on how to surrender they took off walking.

"They've been starved. We fed him after questioning, an MRE. He was too weak to open the food with his hands so he used his teeth. He started eating a cookie and then looked around and found me, offering me half his food. Here was a starving man offering me half his food. I reassured him that it was all his food.

"I can't help but feel sorry for the poor schleps that got drafted into this thing. I think seeing them as real people was harder on me than I thought it would be. War sucks.

"I'm glad I got that off my chest. It's been bugging me all day. But don't think that I'll be slow on the trigger because of the way I feel. Self preservation is still a lot further up than pity. Don't worry. I'm going to walk off the plane when I come home. Probaby run, actually."

"I was fortunate enough to come across the personal sized mirrors your company sent over here to Operation Desert Storm. I'm not sure exactly what route it took to get here. However, most of the things donated go no further than Bahrain or Dahran far south of here. In any event, few things make it up here except for essential logistical resupply items. Quite honestly, we haven't seen ourselves in a mirror for a few months, so the few that made it here were popular items.

"As you probably know, the war is going well for us. Our biggest problem lately has been how to deal with the overwhelming numbers of Iraqis surrendering to us. There are all types of stories lately but the best one so far was the US Marine who got his vehicle stuck in the mud and was pulled out by an Iraqi tank. Then the tank crew surrendered to the Marine. A few more days like that and we will be home free."

The Hale Glass Co. of Anaheim, CA, received this letter from Capt. K. A. Davey, 3rd MA, thanking them for donating some mirrors to the troops. He also mentioned the problems brought on by mass surrenders of the Iraqis.

LaRac Kunz, of Bern, ID, is a clerk-carrier in the Montpelier, ID, Post Office. She shares this description of Christmas in the desert as seen by her brother, Jerry Nelson.

"Dear Mom and Dad. I'm still caught up by the events of last night, Christmas Eve, as the prolonged separation seemed to take its biggest toll yet on individuals in the camp. Most of them are experiencing a remote, isolated Christmas for the first time. We had supper at the usual time, chili dogs, which didn't excite many people. The dining tent folks are busy building Christmas dinner and couldn't put a lot of effort into a lavish Christmas Eve meal.

"After dinner I took a walk through tent city. It's a bit nippy at night now so I have on my flying jacket. Others were about the gravel streets in shorts left over from the 80 degree day and light jackets against the 60 degree night.

"We have street lights but tent city is still made of shadows and ghostly light colored tents with white, talcum powder dust that highlights the wrinkles and the edge of the shadows in the dim light. The bunkers are covered with desert camouflage netting making them cozy patios as well as protection. Small groups of people gather to talk, not much laughter, frequent Merry Christmas greetings as they pass each other.

"As I walk through town on the gravel streets of small chipped stone about four inches deep, my dusty boots sink into the gravel with a crunch that is almost a snow crunch. A tent has a Santa Claus banner covering the door. Behind the netting is a two-foot Christmas tree sitting on a dusty dark green sand bag. No one is around but me and I stand there for five minutes looking at the humble scene that young people who miss home erected. If only I had a picture that could capture the colors, the blinking lights, the Holy Nite it created for me.

"I talked to every person, every gathering I could find, wishing them a Merry Christmas and thanking them for their sacrifice.

"In the rec center there was a crowd around a Christmas TV show, reindeer and Santa puppets. It dawned on me that this was a generation raised on puppet Christmas TV shows. Two large pallets of mail arrived and a box of 'any service member mail' including about 100 frisbees. Before long the dark sky was full of flying frisbees bright white streaks through the star fields.

"I watched the fun until 2000 hours when Col. Joe Emma, the first sergeant and I got a 4 x 4 to visit all those who had to work on Christmas Eve. We went to each security police outpost at dark distant and very quiet place around the perimeter. Each one manned by one person, a couple of them females. I talked with each one for a while, thanking them for what they were doing on Christmas Eve and wished them a Merry Christmas. If only I could capture the lonely setting of the bunker and the bravery I saw in each bunker occupant, I'd send it to every American back home so they could feel the pride I felt.

"I'm proud of these people. I'm proud of the millions of Americans who sent their love and support in letters and boxes of goodies. Despite the lesson, I still miss Christmas with my family."

Not all letters were happy ones. Some romances ended when the partners were separated by thousands of miles. Such was the case with Spec. Paul M. Filek, Jr., of Brookville, IN. Spec. Filek, who still is stationed in Saudi Arabia, wrote his mother about how he felt.

"Well, I finally found out why I haven't heard from Tara. I called her house last night and the first time she hung up on me. The second time I called a guy answered the phone and said: 'She's got a new boyfriend' and hung up. So I think that explains it. That really hurt. I've lost the second girl that I've really cared about. I don't understand why she did that. I guess she couldn't handle my being over here and needed somebody there. I don't know, I'll probably never know. I hope I find my special girl someday.

"Everybody is making it here. Morale is a little low because nobody is getting mail and the boredom. But, we help each other out because we only have each other out here. We are getting real close out here my good friends are getting even better. If one good thing comes out of this it's bringing us closer as a unit.

"I hope we don't get the same treatment that the Vietnam vets got when they came home. I hope the USA is behind us."

"I joined a group for a trip to Jeddah on the Red Sea. It's been wonderful. I've slept on a real bed; eaten shrimp; taken a bath in a bathtub; drank cappucino; shopped; gone snorkeling in the Red Sea; flushed the toilet; and much more. It cost more money than I had to spare but it was worth it.

"During our tour of the city the women were not allowed off the bus unless we had the 'grim reaper' garb. We stopped at a shop and the tour guide collected our money to buy robes and veils for everyone. You should see me! Last night we wore them shopping but saw lots of tourists without. I think our tour guide has a 'business arrangement' with the shop owner. Oh well. It will make a good Halloween outfit."

A chance to visit a Persian Gulf city was one of the fringe benefits of being assigned to the area. Mrs. Bernice Rodgerson, of Richmond, VA, got this description from her daughter Ruth Ann.

Fear was an emotion shared by those on the front lines and those who played a support role. This letter is to his sweetheart from Bill Westerman, an airman on an aircraft carrier.

"About half an hour ago the captain came over the loud speaker to confirm what we already knew. Yesterday the use of force was authorized and we got the go ahead to start our strikes. At 0400 we are launching all of our planes to start our strikes to eliminate Iraq off the face of this planet. This is for real now, honey!

"The morale of the people on this boat is very high. Everyone knew we were going in but nobody knew when. Now that everyone knows we all seem really excited. At least, that is the way everyone tries to show, but I'm sure a lot of them are feeling the same way I am but are just trying to be the man everyone thinks he should be.

"I'm not ashamed to admit it, at least to you, I am scared as hell. Not really for me, but for the pilots and the men on the ground. They are the ones fighting and risking their lives for this just cause. I pray that it will be over quickly and our side will not take too much damages.

"It was kind of funny a lot of the crew was writing messages on the bombs to Iraq. I had to add a saying to one: Roses are Red, Violets are Black, When this bomb hits, No more Iraq."

"I went to a Mass at 1 p.m. It was in a tent. The raindrops would fall through holes in the tent. It was very refreshing and gave us all a spark of hope.

"A chaplain comes around about once a week or so in his vehicle. We just stand around his vehicle and we have a Mass which is pretty much like back home.

"I am writing this letter in a little tent I made with a flashlight. It is pitch dark in here when I turn the flashlight off. I have my headphones on also. I can't wait to get out of here and return home. Everyone here is miserable over the failure of the peace talks. Another demotivator is the fact that we still haven't received any letter mail since we've gotten here. We have gotten packages, but they are nothing compared to letters. Love, Roonie"

"The other day it rained like you wouldn't believe. I took a picture early in the day, I thought everyone would get a kick out of seeing it rain in the desert. Well, by the end of the day I didn't think it was humorous at all.

"About 9 p.m. we had to drive about 50 miles to a new location. It was like driving through a lake. About eight of our trucks got stuck, including mine. A bulldozer had to pull us out. Love, Mickey."

Mrs. Peggy Folse of Raceland, LA, had two sons in the Gulf, with one in the Marines and one in the Army. These are excerpts from their letters to her. The first is from her son Armond Roonie Auten, Jr., in the Marines; the second from her son Mickey Auten in the Army.

"Well I guess its started now. Boy am I glad our planes went out last night and all of them came back. The pilots say they never saw so many bullets in their life. It was such an awesome feeling to see the pilots get out of those planes with a sigh of relief. It made me real proud to be here doing my job.

"The pilots are saying they hit every one of their targets. I put my Stealth T-shirt and my beret in the front landing gear of the Stealth that is next to our sleeping quarters. Hopefully he makes it back safely. Then I am going to have the pilot, Major Boyd, sign my shirt. Something else pretty neat about it is that it will be flown on my birthday. What a neat present."

Souvenirs come in many shapes and sizes. This letter from Sgt. Scott Clemens tells his mother about one he is bringing home with him.

"Hey gang. How's everyone doing back home? If you need me there for anything please don't hesitate to tell the President. I'm doing just fine here actually. I get hot food and hot showers and the Marine Corps has a few stores set up here and about the sand dunes. I live in a tent with a few other Marines from the Dallas unit. We all get along with each other real good as long as they stay on their part of the sand.

"I've got everything I need to make it out here. But, I guess, if you have anything in the store that will keep the sand away I could use it. I doubt you'll have anything like that on the shelf, but if you come across some, go ahead and send two bottles."

Letter from Steve Litzkow from Saudi Arabia to his aunt Jane Gilbert of Irving, TX, and his friends at Mason's Pharmacy.

"I got a letter from my little eight-year-old cousin. She wrote me a cute little letter and then put a PS at the end that says: 'By the way, I've got the chicken pox.' Well, Sarah, I've never had chicken pox before so I got rid of the letter quick and washed my hands with alcohol. Maybe I didn't get anything."

Thomas J. Flammang, historian for the Flammang family in El Paso, TX, writes that in 73 years, one family living in a small rural community in Northwestern Pennsylvania has had three women in the Army Nurse Corps all serving in combat areas. Jo Anne Clare Flammang, daughter of Christopher J. Flammang III, served in Saudi Arabia and Iraq. She writes:

"Looking at these people it is hard to have hatred toward them. They were so very grateful for all that we did. One man just made me cry because he said he had nothing to give me for all that I did. I told him that all I wanted was for him to be well and live in peace. He began to shake his head in agreement and cry and he kissed my hand. Here was a man who probably had nothing left of his home and still wanted to give. These are not people one can hate. They all appeared to be relieved that it was over."

Sarah Martin of Miami, FL, sent seven Christmas cards to "any service member." One of the cards she sent ended up with SRA David M. Fowler. She says she has about 75 letters from him and they have become great friends. This excerpt is from one of his letters to her.

Little things mean a lot in a combat zone. Something as simple as a hot shower was among the dreams of many serving in Operation Desert Storm. Pfc. Jan Jennings, 514th Signal Co., wrote about the problems a female soldier had just trying to keep clean. Her letter is to Mrs. Frances Lewis of Pasadena, CA.

"My name is Jan Jennings. I'm 23 (in six days) and have been in the Army since December 1989. I was assigned to Fort Bragg only a month before we deployed to Saudi Arabia. I've served more time in Saudi Arabia than I have at Fort Bragg. We have been here 91 days.

"We made ourselves our own shower, this way we don't have to walk down the hill, take a shower, then walk back up a hill of sand. We'd never stay clean. Our latrine is down the hill though.

"We haven't had much contact with the Saudis. The ones we do like to stare. They definitely are not used to seeing females in uniform. Their women are full veiled in black so that all you can see is their eyes.

"The MPs here are the ones who work with the Saudi soldiers. So are the pilots flying the jets.

"For me the holiday season is especially hard. It will be the first time away from home. Sure do miss Mom's home cooked meals. We did get the traditional turkey dinner for Thanksgiving and will probably get the same on Christmas. When we get mail every day it feels like Christmas."

"I had the best shower today that I have had since we've been out here. That was about the hardest thing I did today (setting up the shower). I'll tell you why. Our showers are three-man showers with a 500-gallon water tank on top. To warm the water we had to take an emersion heater and put it in the tank. After we got the heater going we have to cover the shower with an old tent liner to block the wind. You got to realize that those showers are just sitting out in the open.

"After that was done I had to wait for the water to warm and the weather to warm up. About 4 p.m. I got my hair cut and then took my shower. It was great!

"...so how is my truck? Did they get the 305 in it? Getting this done isn't costing me an arm and a leg is it? I know how expensive they usually are. Can you send me a picture of my truck?"

Among the things missed most by Spec. Chad Kornelis were hot showers and his truck. He describes the shower problem to his parents, Mr. and Mrs. Phil Kornelis in Everson, WA.

Maintenance crews have an emotional tie to the pilots who fly the planes on which they work. Staff Sgt. Jesse Delao describes this feeling in a letter to Katy Daley of Washington, DC.

"We have been pretty busy flying airplanes 24 hours a day without ever slowing down. I have never in my entire military career seen so many airplanes at this one air base. One after another constantly! Not to mention others that are flying over that are south of us.

"We have been pretty busy with our airplanes by not losing any up until the beginning of this past week. We lost one out of my section and the pilot too. We were all very sad to hear that. Most of us being in maintenance get to know our pilots pretty good. We all hated to hear what had taken place and it was almost like losing a family member. It hit us pretty hard.

"We all know what to expect and realize this is a war and these are the prices we have to pay. I just hope we don't lose any more. We've had several now that have made it back all shot up. One came in two days ago with part of his wing missing and wheel pod.

"The scary part about it was that the right main landing gear tire was also hit and it landed on it. By the time it had come to a complete stop it was worn down to shreds - the tire that is. When the fire department emergency vehicle arrived at the aircraft and got out and looked they took off running away from the aircraft. The pilot did too. What they saw was that a missile was on station next to the wheel pod and wing.

"Well, part of the missile had been hit also and the warhead was exposed. If the missile had been hit less than one inch more it would have exploded. That was a sight to have seen.

"Those Iraqis have some big anti-aircraft artillery (AAAs). We call them triple A's. They just got lucky on this airplane but they sure messed it up good.

"Then, we have this problem with the SCUD missiles that come flying over us. That is one scary feeling I get and the rest of us of course. I'm glad we've got our Patriot missiles to knock them out. They sure light up the night sky and they make a loud boom and rumble. I sometimes see my entire life flash before my eyes. God I sometimes wonder if I'm gonna get to leave this place alive. These SCUDs are some awful big pieces of metal to come raining out of the sky. I usually get in a bunker and take cover pretty fast. Enough of these war stories."

"The only thing I don't like is the damn wind. It very rarely stops and when we're out there and you open your mouth for a second you're chewing sand for the rest of the day. Sure is easy to brush your teeth though. All we do is face into the wind and smile and off comes the socks and the enamel if you stand there too long."

Sgt. Clay Abajian, SOCSENT, managed to preserve his sense of humor while coping with living conditions in the desert. He wrote his mother, Georgia Abajian, in Scottsdale, AZ, about how the sandstorms helped keep his teeth clean.

"We are building POW camps and lots of road work. Yesterday I was watching my grader smooth out the road and put in drainage ditches from my 4 x 4 with a large machine gun as security when a robed man walked up behind my truck with a small boy. The boy made him seem harmless and I greeted him and he spoke fair English.

"I was about 35 miles from any other military so did not remove my M16 from my shoulder at first. Turns out he was only 17 and the boy was his four-year-old nephew. He was wearing a rolex and gold cuff links, very well educated. Spends his summers in Egypt and learned his English in four months while studying in London. Hates Saddam Hussein and likes American soldiers.

"We talked for about 45 minutes and all the while I'm thinking what is he doing in this little hick town across the highway in the middle of nowhere? Strange people.

"He wanted my operators to come over to meet his family and have dinner. If it was just me I'd have done it, but not all three of us. I could see us walking into this little house, four machine guns and almost 500 rounds of ammo. Right! Not to mention the slight language barrier."

War is a business of destruction. It also is a business of building. In this letter to his sister, Kelly Cunningham Dewey, Staff Sgt. James C. Cunningham of the 864th Eng. Bn. tells about building POW camps. The letter was submitted by his grandmother, Myrtle Donahue of Petaluma, CA.

"We finally made it to our hospital site. There is absolutely nothing around here except sand and rocks and it is flat as the eye can see. The trip took us about 10 hours because we were convoying and our drivers were Saudi Arabian. They had to stop along the road twice to pray. Their religion requires them to stop whatever they are doing 5 or 6 times daily to pray. Even businesses close up at prayer time. The women here have to wear the black abayas when they go out in public. Their ankles, arms and hair can't show.

"The evening we arrived the nurses, chief of pharmacy and another pharmacist threw me a surprise birthday party. To get me to the tent I was told the nurses has some pharmacy questions. I was gullible enough to fall for it. I'm glad that I did. The minute I got into the tent they sang happy birthday. We had a MRE and a candle and a crackerjack prize for a present as well as a card signed by everyone."

1st Lt. Stacia Sprigden wrote her parents, Mr. and Mrs. Ray Jones of Grandview, MO, about how Arab religious rites slowed up a convoy. Both she and her husband Staff Sgt. Michael Sprigden are stationed in Germany. She is a pharmacist with the 12th Hospital Evacuation. Both served in the Persian Gulf.

"My men and I will enjoy your gifts for a long time. You've made our Thanksgiving a very special day.

"Thank you personally for the Bible. I have never been very religious but lately I've wanted to understand the word. My roommate has spurred my interest in understanding the Bible. It is hard to come by a copy - the Saudis discourage demonstrations of christianity. Of course the stores do not sell Bibles - the Quran yes, but not the Bible.

"I've been wanting a copy for my own - and here it comes - food for the soul wrapped around food for the body."

Some servicemen found the isolation of the Persian Gulf an inspiration to renew their interest in religion. One example is found in this letter to Donna Douglas of Addison, TX, from Capt. Rich Filippi, an Army intelligence officer.

This letter was written on February 28, 1990, the day the Iraqis surrendered. It came from Lt. Mark Berger to his parents, Eileen and Gerry Berger of White Bear Lake, MN. Mark was a member of the Al-Khanjar Navy-Marine Trauma Center. He, along with about 11 other doctors and 80 corpsmen, provided medical support for the lst Marine Division. Al-Khanjar was the primary casualty receiving station for the First Marines breach operation into Kuwait.

"I woke up this morning to screaming that the Iraqis had surrendered and agreed to comply with the UN resolutions. Thank God it's over.

"The wounded have finally quit flowing in and we are all taking a long breather. We were working 24 hour shifts and, with the helicopters constantly flying overhead, it's tough to get any peaceful rest.

"So far we have treated a total of 330 wounded in action, about 60% of them Iraqi. Fortunately, it was the Iraqis who bore the brunt of the most serious injuries, but several Marines lost their limbs and many had serious facial scars due to artillery and shrapnel. The only Marine death was non-combat related and occured the day before the ground war started when a grenade accidentally was set off. Unbelievable so few were killed, at least on the Allied side. Reports are that over 100,000 Iraqi troops were killed and we have close to 200,000 in POW camps.

"Despite them being the enemy, my heart goes out to a lot of them. One Iraqi captain had graduated from Basra University in 1983 with a computer science degree. Shortly afterwards he was conscripted into service and has been there ever since. He told me his education is now worthless as he has forgotten everything having to serve in the Infantry.

"Another Iraqi POW turned out to be a physician. He was trained at a Moslem university north of Baghdad and was assigned to the Republican Guard. When their unit was overrun he was flown here by helicopter. I ended up admitting him for 'severe constipation' so we could keep him around a few extra days and help us in triage with interpretation. However, when the higher ups found out about him they wanted to interrogate him and he was taken away. As he left he began to weep as he was sure we were going to shoot him."

The rapid end to the war caught many people by surprise. Maj. Anthony Cerri, VIII Airborne Corps, in a letter to his father, Alessio Cerri, had this reaction.

"It was quick. Amazingly so. I still am in partial shock not to mention adrenaline overload. I think that most of our soldiers are the same way. The number of people who thought that it would be this quick could possibly be counted on one hand. I don't think that ANYONE expected our casualties to be as low as they were. While one soldier hurt is too much, we all know that we were lucky. Many (including me) are still wondering what happened to the chemicals.

"There is a possibility that we moved too fast for him to get the munitions to the cannons and the missiles. On the other hand, he may have been worried about our retribution.

"By the way, do you note how I am referring to 'him?' I obviously mean Saddam. Funny thing about all of this is that I don't think the bulk of our soldiers bear any real feelings one way or the other for the average Iraqi soldier. Our hate and fury is reserved for one man, although I could be wrong about this."

"I can't begin to tell you how much your letters of support mean to each of us. It is quite overwhelming to receive letters from people you've never met pledging support and asking if there is anything they can do for you. It certainly is a warm wonderful feeling. It wasn't long ago in this business when the support we recently received was unimaginable.

"The Arab folks down here, (only Charlie Sheen refers to them as ragheads), are quite supportive and very appreciative now that the war is over, they can't seem to do enough for you. For a population which is clearly reserved in their dealings with others, they are flagging people over for pictures and have literally opened their hearts to us.

"We are, of course, very happy this war is now over. Hopefully the Iraqis will get their act together and get rid of Hussein. The world will be a much happier, safer place."

Army Capt. F. Quinn, 930 Sig. Bn., tells Bea Golub of Schaumburg, IL, of Arab reaction to the end of the war.

Lt. Cmdr. Melanie D. Frank, NC, was stationed on board the Hospital Ship Comfort from August of 1990 to April of 1991. She held several different jobs during that period. She worked for the Intensive Care Unit as a staff nurse; she was Charge Nurse of the Light Care Ward (70 beds); and she was Assistant Public Affairs Officer during the days before the ship returned to the United States. During her tour on the ship she kept a daily log of her activities. The log paints a graphic picture of life aboard a hospital ship. She has agreed to share one day's entries with the readers.

"...the sea is all you can see, water, water, water. Jogging on the helo deck and attempting to run the ramps. The ramps are used to take patients from the helo deck down to the casualty receiving wards and into the bowels of the ship.

"I received a shipboard orientation today, tour of the bridge and my gas mask.

"The Military Sealift personnel are quite different and a bit odd. However, they must think that we too are odd. We were told of a possible helo drop of mail on Thursday and that we would be in the Suez Canal on Friday. We also were told that in the Suez Canal we would be receiving casualties. That news, with chemical warfare lectures and us getting our gas masks brought a serious and fearful thought to all of us. Our gas masks were to be put on in five seconds. There is no way we can eat with it on.

"I have this feeling that we may not survive, especially since dehydration is so prevalent in this heat.

"At night we sit around writing letters, writing in our journals and talking to one another. I usually try to go topside around 10 p.m. to check out the stars. Tonight Patty and I went topside to finish our tapes to our hubbies. Bed about midnight."

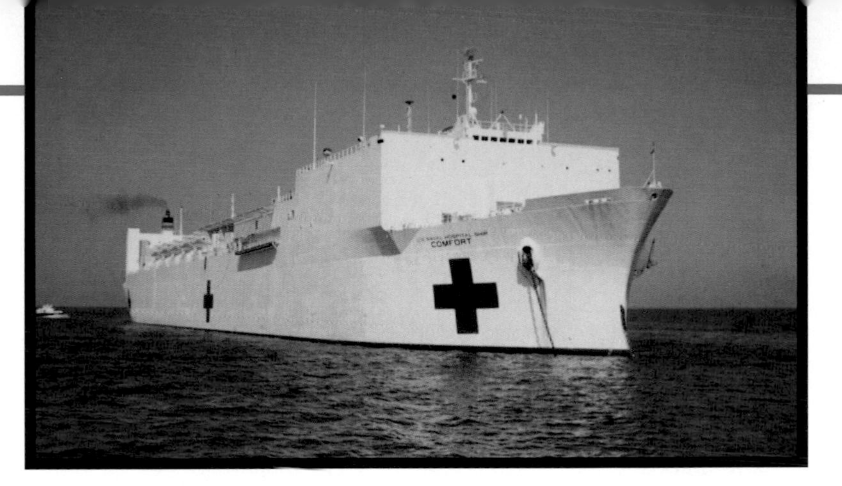

Take a large hospital, equip it with the most modern medical equipment, and staff it with highly trained military and civilian personnel. Prepare it to handle emergency situations under a wide variety of circumstances. Then pack it aboard a ship and sail it to a war area. That is how the United States prepared to handle the heavy casualties it expected to encounter in the Persian Gulf.

Not one but two of these huge floating hospitals, the USNS Comfort and the USNS Mercy, were sent to the Persian Gulf.

Fortunately, the war ended without the expected heavy losses and the ships were able to return home after months in the war zone.

The USNS Comfort is a converted San Clemente class tanker. She was delivered to the Navy on December 1, 1987, and assigned to the Navy Sealift Command to operate. Today's Comfort is crewed by civilian mariners. The Medical Treatment Facility is staffed with medical and non-medical active duty Navy personnel.

Statistics on the size and capability of the ships can only be described as "awesome". Here are a few of them as listed in the brochure provided visitors to the Comfort:

• The USNS Comfort is 894 feet long. That's about the length of three football fields.

• The structure is equivalent to a ten-story building and the distance from the mast to the water line is 124 feet when the ship is fully loaded.

• The ship's cafeteria can feed up to 2,500 people in two hours three times a day. The mess deck seats 500 people at one time.

• Distilling plants on board turn 300,000 gallons of sea water into fresh water each day.

• The laundry facility can clean 56 tons of laundry in a week.

The medical statistics about the Comfort are equally impressive:

• At any given time the ship carries $4.5 million in medical supplies.

• If you unrolled all the gauze on the ship you would have a strip about seven miles long.

• The blood bank on board stores 3,000 units of frozen blood.

Still not impressed? Check this list of some of the medical services on board:

• There are 12 operating rooms, a 20-bed recovery room, a 50-bed Casualty Reception Area and nine elevators for moving patients.

The hospital ships were ready to handle even the heat of the Gulf area. The Comfort has three 400-ton air-conditioning units.

"One thing I really can't wait for is my homecoming. At that time there will be clean sheets, warm showers, good food, fine beers, good looking women, nice clothes and a number of other things. Most of all I will see the family I love so much. There is no measuring how much you all mean to me. You all are the family that I will return to if everything goes right and I use all my resources in this game of survival that's coming up. You all enter my mind every day without fail.

"I now take pride in my service with the Marines. It may help me get through this war. They spent thousands of $ on my gear and weapons and training. It's time for me to earn my money."

Marine Cpl. Rick Tait looks forward to his homecoming in this letter to his sister Patricia L. Tait of Scottsdale, AZ.

This letter from Cpl. Kevin M. Wolfe, of the First Cavalry Division, to his family in Clinton, IA, says it all.

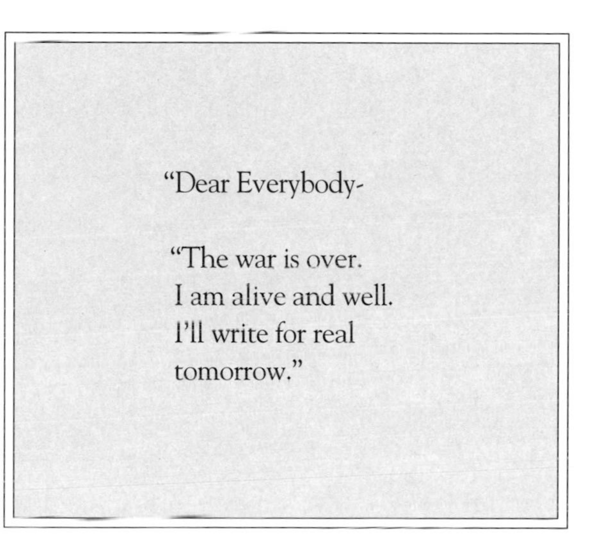

"Dear Everybody-

"The war is over.
I am alive and well.
I'll write for real
tomorrow."

★ VIETNAM ★

The war in Vietnam caused more controversy in the United States than any other military conflict in our history.

With the memory of the Korean War still fresh in their minds, the American people were reluctant to commit to another conflict in a distant land — a land in which war had been a way of life for centuries.

This reluctance was demonstrated in both verbal and physical action as U.S. involvement in the conflict grew. Newspaper editorials and books condemned the war and demanded a U.S. withdrawal. "Draft Dodger" became a household word as young men fled to Canada to escape the draft. Protest rallies were held throughout the country and prominent entertainers and public figures spoke out against continuation of the war.

Demands for an end to the war played a major part in domestic politics throughout the war years. Each election found new candidates claiming they would end the war. A succession of Presidents tried and failed. One, Lyndon Johnson, gave up his quest for re-election when he was unable to end the fighting.

The shooting finally stopped in January 1973 when a peace accord was signed in Paris. This was a war without a winner, a war for which both the military and civilian populations paid a terrible price.

The war left nearly 60,000 Americans dead or missing in action. It produced 238 Medal of Honor winners, the highest tribute the nation can pay to its war heroes.

The greatest impact was on the returning soldiers. Instead of a hero's welcome they were either greeted with scorn or shunned by many who considered the war and the people who fought in it immoral.

It was not until 1980 that Congress authorized a memorial to those who lost their lives in the war. On November 11, 1984, the President accepted the completed memorial on behalf of the nation. The $7 million cost of the memorial was raised entirely through private donations from business and labor organizations. More than 275,000 individual Americans also contributed.

Today a constant stream of visitors moves past the stark black granite walls inscribed with the names of those who gave their lives or are listed as missing in action. Both day and night the lines continue. Some come on crutches, others in wheelchairs. For them the war will never end. These are aging warriors still searching for an inner peace.

Even the most cynical of visitors leave the area with a belief that they could sense the presence of those named on the wall. They leave with a prayer that the sacrifice was not in vain, and for a world in which war would be abandoned as a way to resolve political issues.

Mrs. Mary Douglas, a school teacher in Jacksonville, NC, received this letter from her brother, Staff Sgt. Nolan Drewry, 32, shortly before he was killed near Bon Long, Vietnam, on March 8, 1966. "He was the only uncle my children had and they were too young to remember him," she said.

"I had to leave for Saigon at the drop of a hat. Some equipment came in and I had to fly down and bring it back. The 17th we lost men going out on convoy. Two of them were old buddies of mine I had known for some time. I try and not get too attached to my men as I feel bad more so than usual when one is lost. Not much to write about here except the usual unpleasant things, no more of that. I hope you can read this. My nerves are getting a little shaky. Write when you can. Love, N."

VIETNAM
8 p.m. Sunday night August 28, 1966

My Precious, Darling Ann,

Honey even though I am 12,000 miles away, I do most definitely see the same moon you see except I see it twelve hours before you do, and believe darling I know exactly how you feel when you see the full moon. I also know the feeling of complete satisfaction we both would have if we could have had just one night together, but honey once we're married we'll have the rest of our lives to be alone at night and enjoy the beauty of the full moon.

Probably something you don't know Ann, is that I have every single letter that you've ever written to me also. I know for fact that guys aren't suppose to be sentimental but no one knows how much those letters mean to me, every small detail of our love, the good and bad times, our tempers as well as our tears are also expressed, and darling your so, so right it would be some good reading for our children around the fireplace.

Darling I am so glad you go to the house and keep up with Mom, it makes me feel wonderful and she's always telling me how great she feels when she sees you coming down the walkway. She loves you and knows your wonderful.

Honey, I am glad you know how I feel when I tease you, its just another small way I show you and the world how much I dearly love you and how much I desperately need you for my wife and mine alone. I L-O-V-E you so very much darling and believe you are possitively my one and only love.

Keep my love darling, for it's yours and yours alone - forever. Sleep tight and remember soon I'll be near you, never to leave you again.

John Younkins

"I am about settled here at Lai Khe now, and it is going to be a very interesting assignment. There are 3-4 thousand men here, and many of them are directly involved in combat. I know you've read about the Big Red One — that's us. We are about 23 miles north of Saigon. The men go out on missions, but our closest reminder of the war is the outgoing artillery on our perimeter. The 175 Howitzers sound like they are in our front yard. They sometimes shoot them at night to harass the VC.

"The men are wonderful — all so very considerate and helpful. Of course most of the troops are 18, 19, 20, many are married and all are homesick. Each man can tell you exactly how many days he has left. They really appreciate it when we come by to chat and give them a chance to be recognized as individuals.

"I'm really looking forward to hearing from you. Love, Margaret"

Red Cross girl Margaret Goodrich, of Winston-Salem., NC, based at Lai Khe, swapped a cake for a rifle during a party celebrating the 1st Infantry Division's first year in Vietnam. The Division was protecting Highway 13 for a convoy moving to Saigon so the girls brought the cakes to the men.

Between 1965–1972, the Red Cross sent 627 female college graduates to Vietnam for one year tours to provide mobile recreation programs to combat and combat support troops in forward or otherwise isolated areas. Margaret Goodrich was one of the "Red Cross Girls." She wrote the above letter to her parents on October 3, 1966.

"Hi There Brother,

"Just a few lines to let you know what's happening. Well to start off things are not bad here yet for V.C. activity but I still don't trust this place not one bit. Dad says you are trying to get a job at the telephone co. Well I think that's much better than Dalmo and Arlene says. Walter is waiting for the government to call him, so things should be pretty good. Oh yeah! As you can see I made Sargeant. Dad has bought another car I see. I hope that Chevy did him justice. The mail up here is getting kind of bad. We had a touch of the monsoon season it rained for about ten days and the roads are so bad that no vehicle can get up the mountain. And the mail only comes up with the trucks, sometime a chopper might bring some up. I didn't get my R & R in August so I guess I'll go in September. The days are slowly passing by without a drop I have 120 days but I plan to be home for Thanksgiving if not I'm really going to raise hell. Your car look pretty good so I know I have to get me one now. There really isn't much to say so I'll close now and wish you luck."

Sgt. Clarence Coleman, Team G SBM, Advisory Team # 34, wrote to his brother Ronald in Washington, DC. Ronald also served in Vietnam.

"I don't know how to start this but I will try the best I can. On Nov. 11th Charlie Company was ambushed by a Battalion of N.V.A. I made it out with very minor shrapnel wounds, but many others were not so lucky. We had 9 dead and 62 wounded, several criticaly. I hate to worry you by writing this, but I am sure you have heard or read about this by now and I want you to know I am well. We are back in the Dak To area now, and it is the hottest area in Vietnam.

"We are making contact almost every day, and all of the fire support bases in the area are receiving mortar and ground attacks. Even Dak To is getting mortared regularly. Charlie blows up the ammo dump almost daily and so far has destroyed 2 C-130 aircraft with mortars.

"This is no longer guerilla warfare. It is as conventional as it can get. We are equal in numbers, ammo, supply, & support. We are so close to the Cambodian border (3 miles) that Charlie can get whatever he needs within a matter of hours.

"I have so much work to do it is almost impossible for me to do it all. I am the only man in A,C, or D Companies who can run an L.Z. [Landing Zone] and keep up with everything so I take it daily. It is so busy there I rarely have a chance to eat, and, for instance, last night we didn't get the last wounded out until 11:30. It is very difficult to write but I will do the best I can as often as possible.

"At least I am thankful that the monsoon is over.

"We had a whole bunch of reporters and photogs here the past few days (NBC, CBS, UPI). There should be quite a story out soon. Again, don't worry, I am well and will continue to be so. See you in 6 months. Jack"

Sgt. Jacques deRemer wrote to his parents in Miami, FL, on November 19, 1967, to describe his latest combat experiences in Vietnam.

"This probably won't be in my best handwriting since my right arm is broken & my right elbow is cracked. I don't know if the army let you know that I got busted up a little or not but I did get busted up. It's nothing really serious. It may sound bad as I tell you all the places I have wounds, but I can already walk around a bit & do what I have to do. Well I guess it was a grenade booby-trap that got me. Somebody else stepped on it but it cut up about 4 guys. Don't know how or who they are. Well I already said what my right arm is like. It's a little cut up to but not bad. My left arm is okay, about 10 stitches. About five stitches down the right sideburn of my face. My jaw is broken, but its all wired together, (no problem). I got quite a bit of scrapmetal in the back. One lung had a little cut in it but that's all fixed already, one kidney had a little cut to but every things fine. I know even as I write it, it sounds real bad but, I'm still in one piece and nothing hurts me. I can sleep on my back and nothing hurts. They said the cracked elbow is the worst thing. There'll be lots of scars I suppose but that's about it. They said some of us including me would be evacuated to Japan & probably back to the States soon. I already got my purple heart. That's about it, I don't think I'll have to come back to Nam because he said the elbow will take a real long time to heal. See ya, don't worry cause I'm okay. Love, Von"

Pvt. Vaughn "Von" Bartek, of Company D, 199th Infantry Brigade, wrote from his hospital bed in Saigon on February 26, 1968, to assure his parents back home in Wahoo, NE, that he was okay despite being "busted up."

Dear Folks,

Sorry I haven't been writing, there just isn't time. We had our first inspection today. The company, 61 guys, had 222 demerits. That sounds terrible but it's really only a little above what the average company has on its first inspection. We should start shaping up now. We have a personal inspection Wednesday. The one today was just barracks.

We cross the bridge in a couple weeks. It'll be easier on the other side. We really have to learn a lot in those two weeks.

I still have a bad cold, stuffy nose, lost voice, etc. My blisters are just about healed tho so marching isn't half as bad as it was.

We get our second hair-cut Thursday or Friday. This one is just a trim around the edges. Don't really have any hair yet.

We get to Church at 8:00 Sunday and they have all the sacraments available.

Back to the inspection. Afterwards we had to do 444 jumping jacks and 85 pushups. A lot of guys couldn't make it.

Any news from Von yet? How's everyone? I've got the 2-4 watch in the morning so I won't get much sleep tonite. Can't wait to come home!

Love, Ric

P.S. Could you send some more Air Mail stamps.

One year later, on February 22, 1969, Von's brother, Richard Bartek, was in San Diego undergoing seaman's training preparing for service in the Vietnam theatre.

Sgt. Donald L. Tavener served 25 years in the U.S. Army. He was in the 1st Cavalry Division and the 101st Airborne Division. He was a veteran of World War II, the Korean War, and the Vietnam War. He was assigned to Special Services in Vietnam, arranging entertainment and sports activities for the troops. He wrote frequently to his wife and four children in Anaheim, CA, with illustrations on the envelopes describing his experiences. His family saved 55 envelopes, many of which comprise a framed exhibit for public viewing.

In his last letter before returning home, sent May 26, 1968, Tavener honored Anaheim postal workers with a plaque drawn on the corner of the envelope stating: "AWARD Many thanks to the Postal Dept. for the handling of slightly unorthodox addressed Air Mail."

Tavener died in 1980 at 62.

That [illegible].

I sure hate to leave my troops, but thats the way the cookie crumbles.

Give my love to everyone at home & mom dont worry cause now I'll be home before you know it and all in one piece–

I love you very much

Your Son

Lloyd

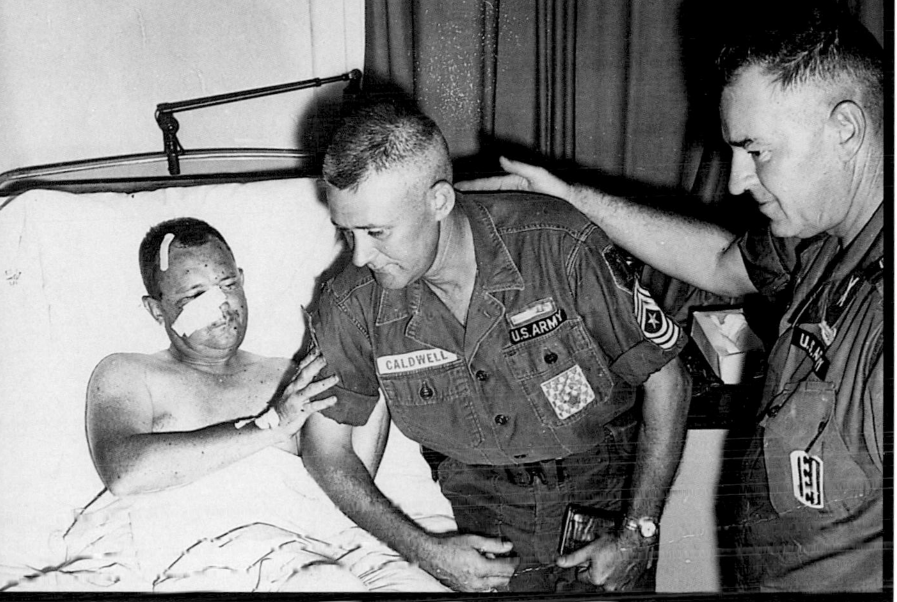

From his hospital bed in Saigon, Lt. Col. Lloyd "Scooter" Burke promoted Sgt. Chandler Caldwell of his unit to Sgt. Maj. Two days earlier, Caldwell saved Burke's life in combat.

One of the unique non-profit organizations in the Nation's Capital is the "Friends of the Vietnam Veterans Memorial" (ZIP Code 20005), which functions largely with the loving help of volunteers. The "Friends" assist Vietnam veterans and their families with specific projects, such as obtaining "name rubbings" of deceased veterans from "The Wall" for persons who cannot make the trip to the city. Another program, "In Touch," tries to link former battle comrades and their families with each other. Thousands of requests are received, hundreds of matches have been made. One such letter was received from schoolteacher Katie Sutherland of Greenwood, MS, whose father, Staff Sgt. Herbert L. Sutherland, was killed in the war.

"I lost my father to the war 6 May 66. I was 8 years old. I didn't realize what death was until I saw my father lying in that casket, so still, quiet and lifeless. It still hurts to know he never came home to us. My father was my whole world. Everything I've done to better myself has been dedicated to his memory.

"The last time I saw my father was Christmas Eve 1965. We had just moved from Ft. Leonard Wood, Missouri (my home town) to Greenwood and gotten settled. It was a cold, snowy night. He was on his way to the airport. Before he left he told my brother, Ralph, 'You are the man of the house now. Take care of your mother and sister till I get back home.' Then he looked at me and said, 'Katie, you'll always be my little girl. Keep your grades up and remember no matter what happens I'll always love you, Flipper (my nickname). You'll always be in my heart.' I've awakened at night with that same dream over and over all these years. I guess I'm lucky, so many children never knew their fathers. I'm just mourning something that remains a memory. So many others are trying to find a little piece of their father that means something to just them.

"I remember Dad writing me (I kept all of the letters) telling me this young man who served under him had a wife back home who was pregnant. He later discovered the child was born the same day the soldier was killed. I never found out the man's name, but Dad said he was a nice guy.

"Well I've poured my heart out enough for one day. I do have a favor to ask of you. Could you go to the 'Wall'whenever you have time and look for S/Sgt Herbert L. Sutherland 6 May 1966. Scratch the name off the wall and send it to me, please. I'd also like to join your organization. Thanks for caring and write me anytime. Katie ('his little girl')".

Vietnam Veterans Memorial USA 20c
ROBERT P SHELLY · DENNIS N HUDSON · STANLEY R TOKARSKI
STEVEN BOAL · BENTON BROWN · GARY W BRUHN
JOSEPH R HAGY Jr · RALPH W JOHNSON · HENRY R LAMBERT
JAMES C McPHILLIPS · HELMUT W PAIER · MAX W PUGMIRE
WILLIAM J SCHUSSLER · VERNON J SEGER · RONALD SOWELL
MELVIN M YAMASHITA · JOSEPH V WHELAN
ALBERT O WAYMAN Jr · THOMAS T FLETCHER
LEE F CLICKNER · MARTIN J CRIBBS · ROBERT J OLLIKAINEN
FLORENCIO Q MARQUEZ · CARL E OLDFIELD · ADRIAN A AKINS
JAMES D STEVENSON · DWIGHT J THORNTON · NEIL S BYNUM
CALVIN BLANTON Jr · JIMMY D BOUDREAUX · JOHN K GOETT
DONALD M DYCE · ROBERT N FUNK · BILLY JOE LEMLEY
CLAUDE B LANDIS II
RAYMOND J KIESLER · RONALD D WESTPHAL
KEITH M PARR · GRAY D WARREN · THOMAS R FOSTER
THOMAS A ENGELMAN · JOE LEE PETERSON
MICHAEL G O'CONNELL · CHARLES E BARNICK
JOHN M McKENNA
THOMAS E CAMPBELL
ARTHUR FOXWORTH
FERMAN B
JAMES A ROBERTS
LAREST C SUTTON
GRAYLAND JONES
CHARLES J ARMSTRONG
ROGER L BYUS
ROGER A DE DIE · REXFORD J
EVERETT GORE Jr
JOHN R NAUGHTON Jr
ROGER B SCHAEFER
TIMOTHY E BADOSTAIN
JERRY L GREENE
ARTHUR J RAMBO
WILLIAM O BRANTLEY Jr
JOHNNY C JONES
JOHNNIE M WAHL · ULYSSES
CARL E DEAN Jr · ROBERT W

KOREA

A small wooden post marks the 38th parallel, the invisible line which separates North and South Korea. The decision of North Korea to cross this line into South Korea in 1950 brought major changes to this ancient Asian land.

Korea had existed for centuries with little need or desire for contact with other countries. Korean history took a sad turn in 1910 when the country was taken over by Japan. It remained under Japanese control until after World War II when it was divided with Russia occupying the North and the United States occupying the South. The United States withdrew from the south when the Republic of Korea was formed.

In 1950 the peaceful existence of this land was shattered when Communist troops from North Korea and China moved south across the 38th parallel. This action touched off a series of events which eventually cost the lives of some 150,000 American troops and nearly one and one half million Koreans. It also led to a clash between a U.S. general and the President of the United States. When the smoke had cleared the career of the general was ended and the long search for peace began.

The United Nations was hesitant about moving against the invaders because they feared this could escalate the Korean conflict into another world war. As an alternative the decision was made to authorize a "police action." This made it possible for member nations to independently send troops to aid South Korea.

American General Douglas MacArthur was named commander of the Allied Forces. He was beginning the fight with several disadvantages stacked against him. Most of his troops were young. Few had been in combat before. They were facing an experienced enemy with large forces and modern weapons. They also had to cope with the devastating heat of a South Korean summer.

The North Koreans exploited their advantage and drove the Allies into a defensive perimeter near the port city of Pusan. The Americans counterattacked from the sea. This attack, plus Allied air support, drove the North Koreans to the Manchurian border.

General MacArthur insisted the Allied forces should pursue the enemy beyond the Manchurian border. He publicly announced that such a strategy would make it possible for all of the troops to be home by Christmas.

The move by MacArthur both surprised and shocked President Truman who was working for a diplomatic solution to the conflict. He ordered MacArthur to refrain from any further foreign policy statements. When the order was ignored, President Truman relieved MacArthur of his command and ordered him back to the United States. MacArthur retired after an emotional speech to the U.S. Congress.

Korea cease-fire talks began in July 1951 and lasted for two years. Fighting ended July 27, 1953.

Army Post Office

Capt. Norman Allan, "I" Company, Fifth Cavalry, wrote in September 1950, to his mother describing combat living conditions in Korea.

"Mother darling: Started again this morning and after 2,000 yards met my vehicles and got a wonderful hot breakfast, our first in nine days—powdered eggs, franks, crackers, coffee, and juice. The enemy has withdrawn...and we are following. Will make contact again soon, probably. Received your letter today with the envelopes and paper. Really grand of you to think of it. Sprained my ankle, same one I got a rock and shrapnel bruise on the other day. It is badly swollen and I can hardly walk, but we have to keep forging ahead. That damn Hill 174 had been taken seven times before our Bn hit the sector. Eleven attacks for a damn rocky, sandy hill. 'L' Company lost over 100 men on it and 'I' lost 80.

" Wish all units were advancing with as little opposition as we have had so far this morning and yesterday afternoon. After such a hard, slow fight it is real nice to be able to push ahead. I will send some souvenirs if I can get them mailed. Have a couple of NK bayonets. It is hard to carry them, particularly when we are taking with us only what's on our backs. Have stripped down to really the minimum—fifty sheets of toilet paper, two pencils, notebook, toothbrush, two brushes and can of oil for my weapon; the rest is weapons, ammo, compass, canteen, shovel, grenades, helmet, field glasses, field jacket, extra pair of socks, map, and one can of cold rations. Captain Curfman always brings me a couple of cans of beer. On the 17th, when he brought his company up to attack through my position, we lay behind a small bush and rock making our plans, enemy bullets snapping six inches overhead, each of us drinking a can of beer. What a war.

"Pretty worried about my ankle, just can hardly stand walking on it but couldn't stand to leave the company for even one day. Holding here now on the side of a little rice paddy while the 7th Cav reconnoiters for a divisional river crossing. So guess we start going again and just as soon keep driving until we hit the 38th Parallel. My lads are all in good spirits but we are tired. Need a barber to get this damn beard off. The division commander says any officer that doesn't shave daily goes to a rifle company. Ha! What can he do to me?

"Haven't had enough water for coffee, let alone shave in, so to hell with them."

6 NOV 1950

HELLO RICHARD:

YOUR MOTHER SAID THAT YOU WERE GOING TO WRITE TO ME SO I WILL DO THE SAME. FIRST OF ALL I HOPE YOU ARE DOING YOUR WORK WELL IN SCHOOL, BECAUSE WHEN I COME HOME SOON I WANT TO SEE A GOOD REPORT CARD FROM YOU, SO KEEP UP YOUR HOMEWORK AND TRY HARD.

THE PICTURE ON TOP IS THE BIG SHIP THAT I AM ON, IT IS VERY FAST AND THEY HAVE A WONDERFUL GANG OF SAILORS THAT CAN REALLY SHOOT THE BIG GUNS. I ALSO WROTE TOMMY A LETTER AND FOR CAROL I SENT HER A LITTLE POEM FROM THE BOYS IN OUR RADIO GANG. TOMMY WILL LET YOU READ HIS LETTER, SO YOU READ THIS LETTER TO TOMMY.

I BET YOU WILL BE SKATING PRETTY SOON NOW, THE WEATHER MUST BE GOOD AND COLD. I WONDER IF YOUR OLD SKATES ARE GOING TO FIT YOU. IF THEY DONT YOU WILL GET A NICE NEW PAIR FOR CHRISTMAS. I HAVE SENT YOU A NICE FANCY JACKET WHICH YOU WILL SOON GET, I HOPE YOU LIKE IT. I AM BRINGING HOME SOME MORE NICE PRESENTS FOR YOU AND THE REST OF THE FAMILY, AND I AM GOING TO BUY SOME MORE THE NEXT TIME WE GO TO JAPAN. RIGHT NOW WE ARE IN KOREA HELPING THE SOLDIERS AND MARINES.

I HOPE YOU LIKE THE COVER ON THIS ENVELOPE SO SAVE YOURS, CAROL'S AND TOMMY FOR ME BECAUSE YOU KNOW I SAVE ALL THOSE COVERS. I WILL MAKE UP SOME MORE FOR YOU NEXT TIME. I HOPE I RECEIVE YOUR LETTER PRETTY SOON, SO I CAN ANSWER IT RIGHT AWAY. GIVE ALL MY LOVE TO YOUR MOTHER AND YOUR SISTER AND BROTHER.

LOVE,

DADDY

Radioman Second Class Louis C. Bakula sent illustrated "covers" to his three young children, Carol, Richard, and Thomas in Peabody, MA, from the USS Rochester during the early months of the Korean War in 1950. Note the Korean War stamp he added years later to one of the letters on the day it was issued. In 1991 he was still an avid stamp and "cover" collector.

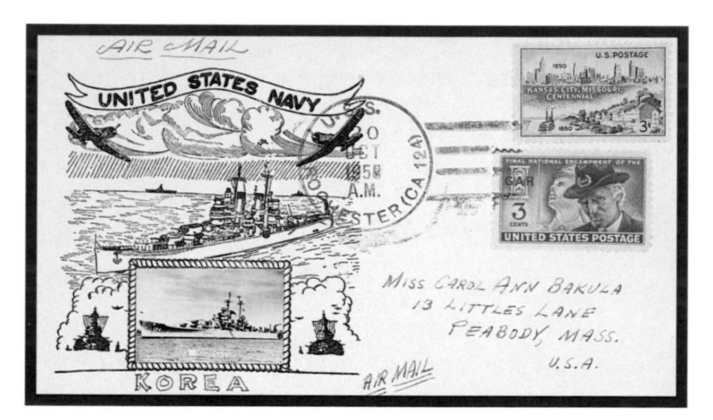

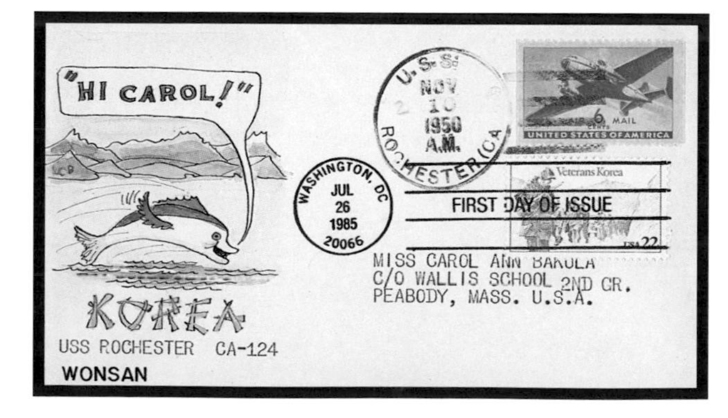

Pvt. James Cardinal, "I" Company, 5th Cavalry Regiment, wrote to his family on December 3, 1950, describing the plight of homeless orphans.

"It's late in the afternoon here in North Korea. I'm on a roadblock with my squad about 11 miles south of Sunchon. The entire army is retreating south. Just how far no one knows, but they're all headed away from the Chinese, who are only about 10 miles away now.

"Everyone, Officers and E.M., admit that we can't hold for long and might have to retreat as far as the 38th parallel. Many of the units streaming thru have been battered severely by the Commies. The 24, 38th and our own 5th Regts. are examples...we don't have enough men, vehicles, equipment or ammunition to fight the Chinks. Even chow is short.

"Anyway no matter what happens I'll take damn good care of myself. They're certainly not going to take me prisoner.

"I feel terribly sorry for the refugees. They seem so miserable & all are hungry & cold. 6 little girls none over 7 years old just came down the road. 3 had no shoes or socks, & they all were homeless orphans. We're letting them sit by the fire & are feeding them. I guess it's all part of the horrors of war. They'll probably wander along till they freeze or starve to death. Joan should see them & then she would appreciate her home, her parents & her school life more than she does.

"Folks, if I get out of this stinking mess alive, you can bet I'll never fight as an infantry-man in a war again. I'm so sick of all the shooting, the death, the smells, the terrible cold & the hunger that I'd give 20 years of my life to be home with you now. But in one way I'm glad I've gone thru it all as one only learns by experience what is good & what is bad for you. Please make Joan understand this so she won't repeat my mistakes.

"I hope to God America never has to undergo what I've seen in Italy & Korea. I'd gladly give my life to spare my family from it.

"Well I hope you're getting those packages out every week. I'll sure be glad when I start getting that peanut butter & Spam, candy & cigarettes. At least I'll have some of the luxuries of America. Keep your spirits up as this will all be over someday & we will all be together again. Until then all my love, Jimmy."

Dearest Mother:

Just a short note to let you know I'm still kicking & to tell you how much I love you.

It has been raining now for 36 hours. Cold too. But I'm making it o.k.

How is everyone at home? Seems like the time has really been dragging by slow over here. The Chinese have really been giving us a battle.

There's really no news here, we're still fighting, but it looks like we may have them just about licked. I sure hope so. Can't ever tell though.

I haven't written lately cause I have not had the time. We've been moving quite a bit.

I wrote to Va to-nite too. How is my son doing? Sure do miss & love him.

Well, Mother don't worry about me I'm safe & sound & I'm well. I'll be home before you know it.

Tell everyone Hello & Thanks to Ann and Jack for the box of candy. It sure was good.

Nite now & I'll write again....Your son who loves you most, Lloyd

Lt. Lloyd L. "Scooter" Burke, Executive Officer of Company G, 5th Cavalry Division, wrote letters to his mother downplaying the daily dangers faced by infantrymen. He explained that he tried to be optimistic and not to worry her. Burke, who served and was wounded both in Korea and Vietnam, was awarded the Medal of Honor, Distinguished Service Cross, Silver Star and Purple Heart before writing this letter on February 1, 1951. He retired from the Army as a colonel.

Pfc. Tommy E. McKinney, Company B, 28th Infantry Regiment, wrote to his sister, Mrs. D. Irene Munns in New Bern, NC, to describe combat in Korea in August 1951.

"I've been on the front lines for the past 4 weeks and I'm a little tired of it by now. I find, sis, that wars are a hell of a mess, I've seen some sights I thought I'd never see, but I did. I've walked a lot further than I thought any man could possibly walk. Sis, I'll tell you the truth. It's hell and I wish I was anywhere but here. I sure would hate to see something like this happen in the states for the children's sake, they're the ones that suffer in a war. You can see that over here. But sis, all in all your Bud is making it o.k. I guess God gifted me with something because no matter how much I walk or how hard we have to drive when we stop at night I always have strength enough to dig in and take care of myself, and that's saying a lot for the hills we have to climb over here, and what they pack on us.

"Sis the kind of people we are fighting over here are not a class to be run down, they are very smart in there way of living, and the Chinese & North Koreans are very good fighters. They are better night fighters than the American G.I. would ever dream of being; they are very sneaky and you have to stay pretty much on the ball. They never come at us in the day time but you can always assure yourself that they will be there at night. They usually hit around midnight or 3 o'clock in the morning and when they attack they come in bunches and they are doped up; they carry some kind of little bottle on them with dope in it. You stay scared over here at night. Man when night comes old Tom really gets ready. Sis I'll give you a little idea of what I have in my foxhole, 2 carbines (rifles), 1 M-1 rifle, 1 Thompson submachine gun known as the burp gun over here, took it off a dead gook, made in Russia; about 200 hand grenades and out in front of my hole I have a bob wire with tin cans on it, booby traps, trip flares, honest sis a mosquito couldn't lite out there (Ha!) and a foxhole buddy. I'm not in as much danger of being hit as some of the fellows are, you see I'm in the morters. It's a heavy weapon, and it stays in the rear. I have 3 rifle platoons in front of me. Over here while your in combat you have to always be thinking. Your thinking about that fellow that's after you, out there somewhere. When your not thinking you get careless, and right then is when old Joe Chinko gets you and believe me Sis, I'm always thinking about that fellow. Sis you do a lot of praying over here. Some of the fellows do some don't. I do, I believe it helps. We have a chaplain and he gives a little sermon when and wherever he can. When it's possible I always attend. Don't let this letter worry you. I just thought I would write you and let you know just how I'm getting along. I believe in letting people know just how it really is. Write soon."

"Arrived in the Frozen Chosen a couple of days ago, the 6th to be exact. Cold as blue blazes.

"We are checking out this week. Seems every group has its policy. We've been flying 80s for 9 months, come over here to fly 80s and they put us through another check out, can't blame them though, they want to know what they are getting in their combat groups...a lot of men depend on one another. It has to be a closely knit team or no one comes back to play again.

"The spirit is fine around here. Mud about two inches deep. Ruts frozen solid at night. Tents cold despite the stove, airmen working long cold hours, pilots flying missions all day long and yet, like every fighter base, not a man would think of shirking his duties. The American fighting man can't be beat, I'm sure of that. One might lose a few battles now and then but never a war. We have inferior aircraft over here, not enough equipment for the pilots; but every man is a 'tiger' and scratch his name from a mission and you've never heard such fuss and hollering.

"The MIGS are really giving the boys a hard time as of the last month. Up to then it was flak and fifties and small arms fire. Now the MIGS are hitting our formations as they come off the target.

"The 80 is no match for the MIG. But our boys have the fighting spirit, no doubt about it. If the MIGS come down the 80s turn into them and put up a scrap. I'm on pins and needles waiting to get a crack at them. Maybe next week. I drove my truck to Yongdong-po yesterday. The destruction is beyond description. Not a hut has been spared. Both sides have occupied this area twice and there 'ain't' nothing left, let me tell you. But the people, the orphans cling to that spark of life somehow living in caves, huts. The homeless kids are the heart rending sight...rain, snow, no place to go, begging, no clothes, maybe a pair of shoes, no socks, little hands blue, bleeding, infected.

"I'll be glad when they call it quits. But while it is on, let me at 'em. Don't worry about me, Dick"

Fighter pilot 1st Lt. Richard E. Cronan, wrote to his mother from Suwon Air Force Base, Korea, on December 8, 1951. Four days later he was killed in action near Kuwah-Ri, North Korea.

Dear Mother and all the family:

Today it seems that we are permitted to write a letter home. In case you do not already know, I am a P.O.W. of the Chinese People's Volunteers. I was allowed to write you late in September, but it is quite possible the letter became lost en route. Fortunately I am in quite good health so you need not worry about me in that respect. Our basic needs are supplied and of course we receive the usual two meals daily. Please give my best regards to Marvin and Roselyn, Walter and Mildred. I am looking forward to seeing you all again before long.

Love,

Fred

First Lt. Frederick P. Pelser, B-26 navigator with the 452nd Bomb Group, U.S. Air Force, was shot down over North Korea on September 17, 1951. This letter of December 24 to his mother in Wickford, RI, was her first notification he was alive. Lt. Pelser (left) was photographed in POW Camp # 2, Pinchong-ni, North Korea in early 1952 with fellow POWs 2nd Lt. Joseph A. Magnant, Warrant Officer Harry Wignall, and 1st Lt. Joseph P. Bednarz (all U.S. Army) by Associated Press photographer Frank Noel, a civilian detainee, captured with some U.S. Marines in 1950. (Noel won a Pulitzer Prize for photography in 1953.) All men were released on September 1, 1953, by which time Pelser received his Captaincy. He was a POW for 711 days.

Pvt. John "Jack" Train, F Company, Seventh Marines, was killed in action shortly after writing this letter on March 30, 1953, to his family in Paw Paw, MI.

"Just a line to let you know I'm safe & well, thank God. In answer to the questions you probably have, yes, I was in the units that were in all the bloody battles of the past 5 days. God, what a slaughter! I am now a combat veteran, and it's not something that I enjoyed becoming. It's something I cannot & will not describe, as I'd rather forget it. Also, I know you'd rather not hear about it, so I'll tell you what has been utmost in my mind the past days of horror — the power of God. Believe me, I prayed as I never have before, and I know God was watching me. Many times I came really close to death, and each time He saved me. Our platoon started out with 38 men to assault & capture a hill. In the morning when we had to give up the hill, there were 10 of us left — I was one of them. He brought me through, so I know your prayers are being heard, but keep them up, I need them now as I never have before.

"This war, and it's a full scale war, regardless of what anyone says, will have to be carried on by the infantrymen, as all the bombs & shells in the world couldn't wipe the Reds out —there are so many of them, like flies.

"I received your letter of March 21, I believe it was, and mail at a time like this boosted my spirits no end, so keep it coming."

Pvt. Louis A. Eberhardt, 4th Mobile Radio Broadcasting Company, wrote to his parents in St. Louis from Seoul, Korea, on Nov. 12, 1953.

Dear Mother and Dad,

I am pleased to hear that you still have a good bit of confidence in me. In the past I haven't done much to inspire confidence, but I am ever so glad to hear that you still believe in me. It means more to me than anything in the world. I shall do, you'll pardon the expression, my damndest to fulfill this confidence.

I've learned a good bit since I've come in the army. I've learned mostly just how little I know. Most of my acquaintances have either fallen into the idiot class, or in the psuedo-intellectual class. The latter is the most disgusting — the idiots can't help it. These so-called intellectuals do nothing but denounce people they feel inferior; inferior because of scanty education, or difference of opinion. For some reason I've been accepted by both groups. I suppose the idiots accept me because I treat them as I feel they should be treated; like human beings. To win the pseudos all I need do is tell them I've been to school, and then, perhaps utter some nothing that seems brilliant to them. The latter I do just to prove to myself how stupid they really are.

I suppose it's a strange note, but the only real people I've met have been — two Jews; Bill Lyfield, and Bernie Gallin, and two negroes; Sam Berry, and Henry Allen. That's why I can't be prejudiced. I believe a man is what he is not because of birth, but rather what he proves himself. Well, that's enough philosophy.

The weather is getting colder here — it was about twenty eight this morning. Have you gotten any snow yet? I sure would love to be home. I love snow, and ice — that is, at home. I don't think I'm going to like it here. Remember Christmas fifty-one?...all that ice? I hope it does the same thing next Christmas when I'm home.

Love, Your son, Lou

1939–1945

☆ WORLD ☆ WAR ☆ II ☆

Mention World War II to the Persian Gulf fighters and you may draw a blank look. For them that war was history before they were born. But, ask their grandfathers about war and they will assure you that this was "The Great War" and everything that came before or followed never quite measured up.

There is some justification for their claim. World War II changed the way all future wars would be fought. Air power became a key factor in the movement of troops and supplies. It made it possible to move large numbers of troops and large amounts of supplies a great distance in a short time. At the same time the Navy was expanding its forces and its capabilities. Giant aircraft carriers dotted the ocean and made it possible for fighters and bombers to reach their targets in short order.

Dropping the atomic bomb is probably the most remembered news of the war. It made the aggressors pay a terrible price in the destruction of their land and its people. This was a more horrible weapon than man had ever used before. While the atomic bomb left carnage and death in its wake, the war also is remembered for what happened afterward: the development of the Marshall Plan, which made possible the rebuilding of Europe and laid the groundwork for peace for many years.

World War II was actually several different wars–wars that were worlds apart in their location and the way in which they had to be fought. In Europe the fighting was in the city streets and surrounding areas. Sometimes the troops had to fight from house to house as they drove the Axis powers back to their home grounds and ultimate defeat.

The Pacific campaign required the troops to fight not only the military enemy but the natural one as well. In the Pacific the natural enemy was moisture. Weapons rusted overnight and water rose in the foxholes almost as soon as they were dug.

The jungle was thick and tough and the heavy rains made paths disappear a few days after machetes carved them from the wilderness. The troops also had to fight against disease. Malaria was waiting in a mosquito bite and mysterious tropical diseases threatened those who were tempted to take a bath in some standing water.

Conditions in Africa perhaps came the closest to those encountered in the Persian Gulf. Water was at a premium and had to be conserved. In Africa the troops also had to cope with sand in their weapons, in their food, and in their lives.

ARMY
"KEEP 'EM FLYING
IS OUR BATTLE CRY!
AVIATION CADETS.....
Young Men, 18 to 26 Years
of Age Inclusive, for Air Crew
Training as Bombardiers,
Navigators and Pilots.
Victory
INDUCTION STATION
THE FLAG
of the United States of America

Letters sent home by the troops described in dramatic detail the progress on each of the fronts. For the most part the war was supported by the American people, providing a major morale booster to the troops. Families with a son or daughter in the service placed silver stars in their windows. If a serviceman died in battle, the star was replaced by one colored gold. Thus, Gold Star Mothers shared with the community a sad reminder of the horrible cost of war in human lives.

Gen. Dwight David Eisenhower wrote a birthday letter to his wife, Mamie, from London on or about October 30, 1942, and asked her not to open it until November 14.

"By the time you read this your newspapers will probably have told you where I am and you will understand why your birthday letter had to be written some time in advance. You will also realize that I have been busy—very busy—and any lapse in the arrival of letters will be explained to you. Knowing that all this will be plain to you by the time you read this I am not compelled to violate rules of secrecy and censorship in order to tell you what I am planning to do.

"I hope you won't be disturbed or worried. War inevitably carries its risks to life and limb—but the chances, in my case, are all in my favor—a fact which you must always remember. Moreover—even if the worst should ever happen to me, please don't be too upset. In 31 years as a soldier I've been exposed to few of the risks that most have encountered. If I had been in the Theatre of Operations during the World War I, I might easily have long since been gone. And, while I don't mean to be fatalistic or too philosophical—I truly feel that what the U.S. and the world are facing today is so much bigger than anyone of us can even comprehend, that personal sacrifice and loss must not be allowed to overwhelm any of us.

"Anyway—on the day you open this letter you'll be 46. I'd like to be there to help you celebrate, and to kiss you 46 times (multiplied by any number you care to pick). I imagine Ruth will have some little party for you, or maybe Helen & Milton will try to get hold of you. In any event I will be with you in thought, and entirely aside from the usual congratulations and felicitations, I will be thinking with the deepest gratitude of the many happy hours and years you've given me. I'm quite aware of the fact that I'm not always easy

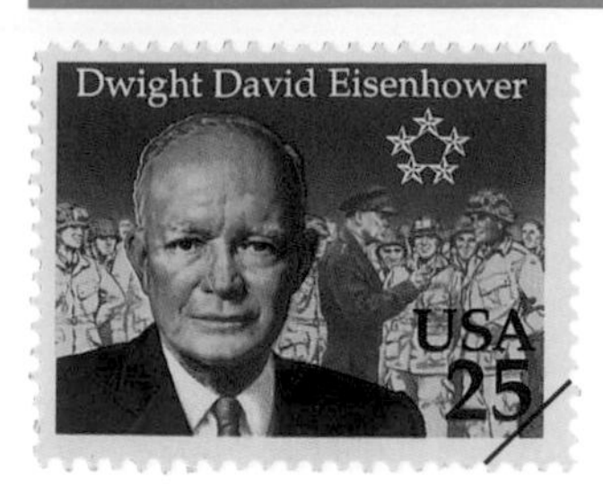

to live with—that frequently I'm irascible and even mean—and my gratitude is even greater when I realize how often you've put up with me in spite of such traits.

"The crowning thing you've given me is our son—he has been so wonderful, unquestionably because he's so much you—that I find I live in him so very often. Your love and our son have been my greatest gifts from life, and on your birthday I wish that my powers of expression were such as to make you understand that thoroughly—clearly and for always. I've never wanted any other wife—you're mine, and for that reason I've been luckier than any other man.

"I feel this war is so big—so vast—that my mind completely refuses to visualize anything beyond its possible end. But I do hope that all through it I do my duty so well, so efficiently, that regardless of what may happen to me you and John can always be proud that we three are one family. I do not seek rank—I don't even seek acclaim, because it is easily possible that a commander can receive credit (and blame) for which he is no ways responsible. But if my own conscience tells me I've done my duty—I will always come back to you in the certainty that you'd understand any fall from the high places, and that my place in your heart would be as big as ever.

"Again—love and kisses on your birthday!"

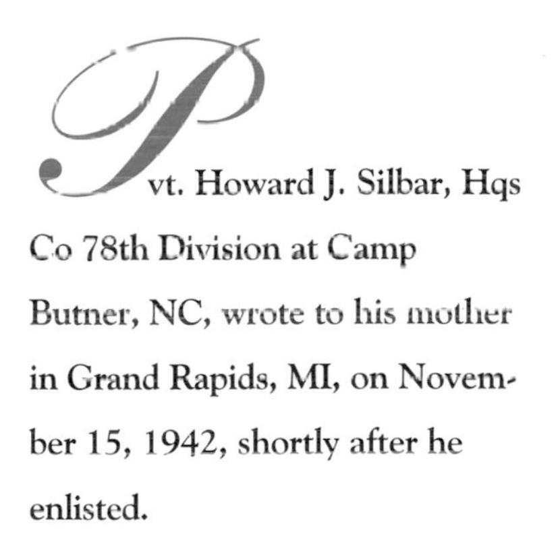

vt. Howard J. Silbar, Hqs Co 78th Division at Camp Butner, NC, wrote to his mother in Grand Rapids, MI, on November 15, 1942, shortly after he enlisted.

"Now for the moral of this letter, let me say that if there's anything that may eventually drive me into officers training school it will be the grovelling that I have to do before these officers that I must constantly deal with at headquarters. When any of the generals or colonels even walk into our shoe-box office to see the captain, work and breathing stop and we spring to attention. I must 'Yessir' and 'Nosir' until I could choke. Why would you believe it I had a hamburg in Raleigh last nite while waiting for the bus connection, & when the waitress (a charming thing) said to me, 'Will you have mustard?' I replied 'Yessir'—even to her."

Three years later, now Maj. Howard J. Silbar, Supply and Administrative Officer, Public Relations Division, Wiesbaden, Germany, wrote to his Aunt Bert in Grand Rapids, MI, on September 23, 1945.

"Today I saw Darmstadt. I did no fraternizing, naturally—and I believe perhaps on this line of geneology, we are safe in saying that the past is completely buried. Any skeletons any of us might be harboring will rattle no longer in Darmstadt, because there aren't any closets for them to rattle in. If any of our family survived the pogroms, they certainly survived neither the terrific bombing nor the shell fire. Darmstadt, like our forefathers, is dead and turning to dust. There are so few people left in the town that the rubble still isn't cleared from the street.

"Every time I see a wrecked city, I think how tired I am of seeing wrecked cities. Basically they all look alike — no roofs, gutted houses, empty stone walls, chimneys, and footpaths only down the wide streets. I'm still amazed however at the colossal bankruptcy of the entire German civilization and everything that goes to make up a modern society of humans. If we work on the premise that normal humans don't deserve such catastrophe, the logic follows that perhaps the Germans as a nation are not normal. So I saw nothing in Darmstadt that I could point to in pride as being the Old Massa's Homestead; nor did I see anything that I could be ashamed of."

Dispatch of March 10, 1943 ....

"Is War dramatic, or isn't it? Certainly there are great tragedies, unbelievable stories, even a constant undertone of comedy. It is the job of us writers to transfer all that drama back to you folks at home. Most of the correspondents have the ability to do it. But when I sit down to write, here is what I see instead: Men at the front suffering and wishing they were somewhere else, men in routine jobs just behind the lines bellyaching because they can't get to the front, all of them desperately hungry for somebody to talk to besides themselves, no women to be heroes in front of, damn little wine to drink, precious little song, cold and fairly dirty, just toiling from day to day in a world full of insecurity, discomfort, homesickness and a dulled sense of danger..."

North Africa, May 3, 1943 (on the front lines before Mateur)

"Word is passed that mail will be collected that evening, so the boys sit on the ground and write letters. But writing is hard, for they can't tell in their letters what they've been through."

With penetrating insight, journalist Ernie Pyle and editorial cartoonist Bill Mauldin brought World War II as experienced by its soldiers into millions of Americans' homes through daily newspapers. Pyle and Mauldin lived with the combatants, suffering the same misery, loneliness, pain, and anxiety and reporting it honestly. They brought into sharp focus the brotherhood of soldiers in battle and their courage facing known and unknown horrors. Later wars would be brought instantly and electronically to the nation's television screens, but this war's story was reported chiefly by printed word, picture, radio broadcasts, and newsreel.

Ernie Pyle wrote dispatches from North Africa and Europe and was then sent to the Pacific theatre. He was killed by a Japanese sniper on Ie Shima on April 18, 1945 — two days after the Marines he accompanied landed on the island and twenty days before the Germans surrendered in Europe.

Mauldin returned safely from the war and settled in New Mexico where he continued drawing his editorial cartoons and took up sculpture.

Both received journalism's most coveted Pulitzer Prize for their superb talents. Ernie Pyle was further honored by the U.S. Postal Service in 1971 with the issuance of a postage stamp.

"My son. Five days old. Good-lookin' kid, ain't he?"

Dear Mother and Dad

Have been so busy that I haven't had a bit of time to write. Have two of my combat crews on leave so have been flying practically all the time. Shouldn't have given them leave at the same time but they were due and tried to keep them all happy.

We have new B 25Ds. They are a much nicer ship than the B 34 and have a much longer cruising range. We are doing six hour patrols now and sometimes eight. Don't know when we will get B 24s but expect they will be arriving sometime this summer.

Write when you can and please try to understand that I haven't been neglecting writing because I wanted to; its just been that I can't find a minute's time. Hope that you are all in good health.

Love, John

First Lt. John S. Dreher and his crew from the 16th Bomb Squadron based at Charleston, SC, Army Air Base, lost their lives on anti-submarine dawn patrol on May 18, 1943.

My Dear Mr. Drummond:

I rejoice with you that news has come of Ace. Before my letter cleared channels in answer to your letter, we had news from the States that he was a Prisoner of War. I know that you are still anxious, but it is a great comfort to know that he is alive and we trust well.

The International Red Cross reports that the PWs are well treated, and I think for you it will be but a question of time before Ace returns to you safe and sound. We rejoice that it has worked out so, and pray that it might not be too long now.

Perhaps he is safer where he is than he would be here, but knowing Ace as well as I do, I know he would want to be here with the rest of us doing his job. We're so glad for the news, for we thought a lot of him, and were sorry when he went down, though we were reasonably sure he was safe.

I wish I could write to every parent with as good news as this. War is not pleasant, and it lightens my heart to have a note like this (even with the mistakes this old typewriter makes!) go out from this office.

Most sincerely yours,

Frank J. Landolt, Chaplain
405th Fighter Group

Christmas, 1944

Dear Mom, Dad & All,

I wish you all a Merry Christmas & a Happy New Year. I know it's impossible for me to be with you all but maybe next year we'll all be together. Thanks to the American Red Cross we're having a very nice dinner. We'll never forget this wonderful organization. I also received the most wonderful Christmas gift any one ever received! two letters from home! My first ones too. Lib, I think I enjoyed those words more than I have ever enjoyed anything before in all my life....Tell all I said "hello" & hope to see them again soon....Mom, Dad don't worry for I'm o.k. & hope to see you soon,

Love, Your son, John,

First Lt. John W. Drummond

The parents of fighter pilot 1st Lt. John W. Drummond, of Ninety-Six, SC, first learned he was alive and safe in a prison camp in Germany in a letter written on October 6, 1944, by Chaplain Frank J. Landolt, 405th Fighter Group. Drummond wrote to his family on Christmas Day, 1944, to reassure them he was well. He was a POW for 10 months.

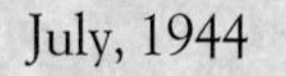

Arnold Rahe was killed in action in France on July 25, 1944.

July, 1944

Dear Mother and Dad,

Strange thing about this letter; if I am alive a month from now you will not receive it, for its coming to you will mean that after my twenty-sixth birthday God has decided I've been on earth long enough and He wants me to come up and take the examination for permanent service with Him. It's hard to write a letter like this; there are a million and one things I want to say; there are so many I ought to say if this is the last letter that I can ever write to you. I'm telling you that I love you two so very much; not one better than the other but absolutely equally. Some things a man can never thank his parents enough for; they come to be taken for granted through the years: care when you are a child, and countless favors as he grows up. I am recalling now all your prayers, your watchfulness — all the sacrifices that were made for me when sacrifice was a real thing and not just a word to be used in speeches. I know how you had to do without things to put me through school. You thought I didn't realize these things, but I did.

For any and all grief I've caused you in those twenty-six years, I'm most heartily sorry. I know that I can never make up for those little hurts and real wounds, but maybe if God permits me to be with Him above, I can help out there. It's a funny thing about this mission, but I don't think I'll come back alive. Call it an Irishman's hunch or presentiment or whatever you will. I believe it is Our Lord and His Blessed Mother giving me a tip to be prepared. In the event I am killed, you can have the consolation of knowing that it was in the "line of duty" to my country. I am saddened because I shall not be with you in your life's later years, but until we meet I want you to know that I die as I tried to live, the way you taught me. Life has turned out different from the way we planned it, and at twenty-six I die with many things to live for, but the loss of the few remaining years unlived together is as nothing compared to the eternity to which we go, and it will be well worth while if I give my life to help cure a sickened world, and if you and I can help to spare other mothers and fathers and younger generations from the griefs of war.

As I prepare for this last mission, I am a bit homesick. I have been at other times when I thought of you, when I lost a friend, when I wondered when and how this war would end. But the whole world is homesick! I have never written like this before, even though I have been through the "valley of the shadows" many times, but this night, Mother and Dad, you are very close to me and I long so to talk to you. I think of you and of home. America has asked much of our generation, but I am glad to give her all I have because she has given me so much.

Goodnight, dear Mother and Dad. God love you. Your loving son,

(Bud) Arnold Rahe

Bombardier Lt. Joseph L. Johnson of the 100th Squadron, 42nd Group, was shot down on a mission over the Pacific island of Palawan one month after he wrote to Bette Kamm of Ashland, WI, on March 11, 1945.

"You're probably wondering where I'm writing from. Unfortunately I can't say except somewhere in the Netherlands Indies (East). I was down in New Guinea awhile, and moved up here shortly after.

"I'm with a medium bombardment outfit flying in B-25's. Generally they're considered a pretty safe ship. Naturally there are exceptions.

"One of those tropical downpours started a few minutes ago. Practically flattens you if you're out in it. We get most of our water except drinking from the rains. And do they come.

"Down in New Guinea the natives are definitely the Negroid type, but up here they have a large admixture of Polynesian blood. The native women's beauty will never be the cause of any unfaithfulness around here though. Unfortunately.

"We get beer once in awhile, some gin, a little brandy and rum and after each mission a shot of bourbon, that great old morale builder. No Scotch, however that's not to great a hardship since we have a harder time getting the mixings than we do the alcohol.

"Believe it or not, chess is the rage in and around the tent area. I played a bit in the States, but over here we're really concentrating. Some substitute for the fair sex, but when they're not around you'ld be surprised at the adjustments one can make.

"There are a few Red Cross workers & nurses. Every guy in the place from the Colonel on down is mentally undressing them whenever they appear and do they know it.

"I've been answering some of the enlisted men's mail to their families and woman you ought to hear those guys talk. I thought "Forever Amber" was it.

"Put the old clamp on your love life woman until I get back to complete our Unfinished Symphony."

"For the past week we have been quite busy with no chance to write. Memorial Day we played the ceremony at Margraten Cemetery near Maastricht, Holland. General Simpson (three stars) and a dozen brass hats attended. It is the 9th Army cemetery with about 14,000 graves. A 21-gun salute was fired after a short talk by General Simpson.

"Although it is my fifth time across the Rhine and the Ruhr valley I still had the same sickening feeling the destruction in that area gave me the first trip. Saw the famous dragon's teeth and pill-boxes before Aachen; also what is left of the Krupp works at Essen. That is the kind of destruction I am in favor of however.

"Don't know what is in store for us, but have a feeling we will see more of Germany before leaving Europe. The Germans are now busy courting our good will. The youngsters, no doubt under orders, wave and smile when we pass but none of the old-timers pays any attention to them. Yet, if you turn your back or leave anything unguarded it promptly disappears.

"In contrast to the local scene, the situation at Maastricht is almost reminiscent of peace-time. Outside of a few blown bridges and broken windows the town in appearance seems untouched by war. The many colored brick houses with freshly scrubbed door-ways, civilian automobiles, store windows attractively decorated although short on merchandise, and the general briskness of the shoppers makes a picture quite different from the usual one of destruction and despair."

Musician

Robert D. Shaffer, who served with Gen. Patton's Army and played in the 35th Division Army Band, wrote to his mother in Fostoria, OH, on May 31, 1945, from Recklinghausen, Germany.

"Dear, the news today was really quite startling to everyone. The new bomb is practically unbelievable, and to think that that was what was going on there at Hanford practically in our own back yard. That Admiral must have known about the bomb when he made his statement that the next invasion the men could go ashore standing up. That suits this rear area commando. I don't like crawling on my belly nohow. ha! Think of the new field this atomic bomb has opened up. They have been trying for many years to harness the atom and have finally succeeded. There will be millions of peace time uses from this invention. This war has brought about startling changes. During your and my life Honey we will see things that our own folks wouldn't believe.

"Aviation will be as commonplace as autos. Our generation will live in a world of speed & industries that have never before been engaged in...."

And on August 8, he wrote:

"Just think, one the size of a pea will blow a crater large enough to put a 6 room house in. The Japs had sure better be making up their minds whether they want to die or continue to live under our domination. Dearest I'm sure we are closer to the time of our reunion than either of us think."

Pvt. Joseph Q. Adams, 43rd Replacement Depot, 6th Army, wrote to his wife in Grandview, WA, about the atom bomb from the South Pacific on August 7, 1945.

Capt. Ralph T. Noonan of the 101st Quartermaster Regiment stationed at New Caledonia, South Pacific, wrote to his wife on July 19, 1942.

"Had some experience last night. Joe Berkowitz invited about 10 natives up to the house to sing and dance for us. The chant sounds similar to our church hymns, and they all had beautiful voices. They really went native when they started to dance. And it wasn't difficult to realize that some of these people were head-hunters less than 30 years ago. For music they used an empty box upside down; they beat this box with two pieces of stone to produce a weird music. Used a type of shuffling step that looked like some of Tommy's dancing in front of the radio. As the tempo increased they really went to town, swinging clubs, and yelling for all they had in them. Normally they keep it up for hours until they drop from exhaustion. In many ways they are nothing but children. They'll work their hands off for the Americans but have little use for the French. Give them an American cigarette and they will work all day....Most of them are big fellows and will work like horses but for some reason they seem to get sick very easy. After a cold spell we have a bunch of them sick....You should see them parading around the streets dressed in our heavy underwear, a pair of overshoes, and one of those winter hats you didn't like. Then they have another favorite hat—a flour bag. And the more flour that they get over themselves the better they like it. Then again you'll see them decked out in all kinds of flowers and branches. Just like little kids."

UNITED STATES POSTAGE
3¢

My Dear Joe,

Today, we received your letter of Tuesday, Feb. 13. Dear, we also saw in the papers, the news, that the 5th Division is attacking Iwo Jima—and since the moment I read it, I have prayed constantly that you will emerge from it unharmed. I know you will, dear—God has shown me many times, especially recently, that He loves my children, and is with them every moment.

Remember dear, I'll always love you—always, always. God love you and be with you every minute. Good night, my little Joey,

Mother

Mrs. W.R. McDonald, of Cincinnati, OH, wrote to her son, Marine Corps Pfc. Joseph T. McDonald, 1st Bn., 27th Marines, 5th Division, on Monday, February 19, 1945.

On Sunday, April 15, 1945, Joe wrote to his parents from rest camp to describe his Iwo Jima experience:

"Well, here we are, back 'home' again for a much-needed rest. Just as soon as I can I will send a package which will include the few 'trinkets' I picked up on Iwo. I am making a bracelet out of aluminum from a Jap plane shot down on Iwo, for Mary Ellen and also a scarf for Clair which will be made out of one of the silk parachute flares which were used to illuminate the areas at night to prevent the 'gooks' from sneaking in on us.

"We who hit on D-Day and lived through the affair in its entirety were guided by the hand of God. I know I was—every single night that I was there I prayed in gratitude to God for His protection during that day. I said your 'special prayer,' Mom, frequently during each day and night. So I'm certain your prayers were responsible for my safety.

"On D-Day plus three we moved our C.P. into a steep revetment which was formerly used by the Japs to hide their planes from our attacks. This revetment was just behind airfield # 2. Well apparently the Nips on the higher ground were 'zeroed in' on this position with their artillery and mortars because not long after we moved in they concentrated a terrific barrage on us. I was lying in a shallow hole with another fellow, and just to the side of me I had set my radio and other gear. In front of me were two other friends, and to the other side close by were still two more. Well three terrific explosions went off right behind us, very close, so close that we were sprayed by small pieces of earth and steel. These shots were about thirty seconds apart. All of a sudden, on impulse, I yelled to 'so-&-so' that I was going to make a run for the top of the hill towards where the firing was coming from. I waited for one more to hit and then I stood up and ran. I reached a spot about ten yards away I turned around to see another big explosion even closer to the spot I had just vacated. I scampered up the short, steep hill and dove in on a hole which contained three other guys.

"Two hours later, when the barrage subsided we went back down to see what damage had been done. I found all my gear shattered with cuts, the radio also. I also learned that all the guys who had been laying around me were wounded and had already been evacuated to the rear! And the explosion which had done it was the one immediately following my departure from that spot. What possessed me to leave when I did, I'll never know. But certainly it was Divine Providence which took my hand and led me from there just a few seconds soon enough to escape being hit.

"There were many other close-shaves for all of us, most of them on the beach. Most of us have only a dazed memory of the beach at the time we hit. I recall that just after we were on it a shell hit right behind Willie and I and showered us with earth and spent fragments. I turned to look at him and it was so smoky and dusty that I couldn't see him. When I finally did it was to find that a fragment had gone through his canteen, and also through every section of radio aerial he had carried beside him! And he wasn't touched, except for a scratched knee.

"Our battalion lost scores of the original men whom we hit with, and also many replacements besides. When we look around now we see very few familiar faces especially in our line companys A, B, and C. Our Hqs. Co was hit hard in comparison to others and, as you prophesized, many good friends made the supreme sacrifice. These we visited the day before we left the island where they dedicated the 5th Div cemetery on Iwo. It was an impressive ceremony and the cemetery is really beautiful considering that it was built not far from places where things were going 'fast and furious.'

"So until tomorrow, God bless you all, lots and lots of love from your son Joe."

Japan's Foreign Minister Mamoru Shigemitzu was the first to sign the surrender document ending World War II in the Pacific theatre. The ceremonies were held on board the U.S. Battleship Missouri on September 2, 1945, in Tokyo Bay.

Gen. of the Army Douglas MacArthur then signed for all the Allied Powers (Great Britain, China, France, Soviet Union, Australia, Canada, the Netherlands and New Zealand). Fleet Adm. Chester R. Nimitz (seated) signed the document for the United States. Adms. William Frederick Halsey, Vice Adm. Frederick C. Sherman, Rear Adm. Forrest P. Sherman, U.S. Lt. Gen. Jonathan Wainwright and British Lt. Gen. Sir Arthur Percival also attended.

n the day of the Japanese surrender signing ceremony, Adm. Chester R. Nimitz retired to his cabin to write his daily letter to his wife, Catherine. He wrote it on the back of the printed program of the surrender document.

September 2, 1945

"Best Beloved, The big moment is over and the Japs have signed the formal terms of surrender. Everything clicked in a minute—Tokyo Time. The press came off in a transport destroyer before 8 A.M., followed by another destroyer carrying all the guests except the Supreme Commander's private party, which came alongside as did all the destroyers at 8:30. I don't see how I can describe this scene or why I should attempt it, because there were present at least 200 correspondents who have by now written and broadcast thousands of words of description, which even as I write at 11:30 A.M. is either being read or heard by you and all our children, wherever they may be. Many of our officers from the ships still at sea were present, they having been flown in by plane. Among those was Shafroth, who particularly asked that I include in this letter his best wishes to you and Mary. Fortunately the bad weather for the last two days passed on, and we were blessed with dry, though overcast, skies.

"Last night I was tremendously pleased and surprised to receive your fine letters of the 23rd and 24th of August with the enclosures, which were brought up from Guam by one of our officers who brought up important mail. This is rapid time for your 24th August letter, written on my 25th, with only seven days from Berkeley to Tokyo Bay.

"Now I must close. All my heart's devotion.
Love and kisses to my sweetheart."

(Every turret top, every point of vantage was occupied by newsmen, cameramen, including local Japanese papers, and officers and men from the ship who could get a foothold. When it came time to sign, I confess to nervous excitement, but I did sign in the correct places. One signer did not. First copy signed with the Woo gold gift pen, and the second copy signed with my old green Parker pen.)

Mrs. Nimitz later explained: "The pen which he called the Woo pen was given to him by our friends Y.C. and Eching Woo, great friends of ours. And the other was a 50-cent Parker pen that he bought from a bumboat in our travels. That is now in the Naval Academy Museum."

V-MAIL 1942-1945

Anyone who has studied the history of World War II will have seen photos of Winston Churchill, Prime Minister of Great Britain at that time. Undoubtedly the most famous of those photos is the one showing him with his right hand held high, his fingers spread to form a V. The gesture was recognized everywhere as the V for Victory sign that would signal the eventual defeat of the Germans and their allies.

There was another V to come out of that war, and it, too, played a major role in keeping high the morale of the troops fighting far from home. This was the V-Mail letter, designed to meet a most pressing need and to meet it in an amazingly successful fashion.

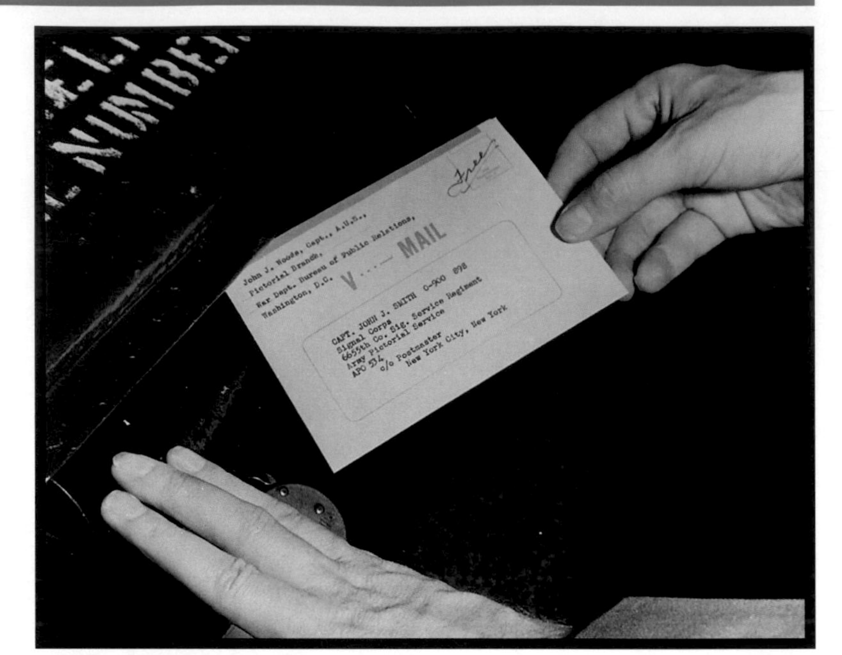

All I WANT FOR Christmas IS You!

During the early years of the war there was a shortage of ships and planes needed to carry the troops and their supplies to the battlefront. Only the most essential items could be carried. The rest waited for slow freighters or widely scattered airplane flights to complete the mission.

One of the first casualties was the mail from home. With millions of troops overseas waiting for letters from home, the transportation facilities were strained to the limit. Sometimes mail sacks would have to wait until there was room on a later supply ship. The scenario had the makings of a major downer for morale.

Postal Service historians say the solution came with the introduction of V-Mail on June 15, 1942. This new service made it possible to transmit letters on microfilm to and from members of the armed forces overseas.

V-Mail, a combination letter and envelope on distinctive and uniform stationery, was accorded preferential treatment in processing and moving, thus cutting the time it took for letters to reach the troops.

The V-Mail sheet provided space on one side for a message and instructions for sending the letter on the reverse. Users were told to use dark ink and to keep the message in the alloted space so that it could be photographed. Originally no enclosures were allowed. Later an exception was made to permit sending pictures of infants under a year old or children born after the service man left for overseas.

V-Mail processing stations were set up in the United States and overseas. At these stations the letters were opened by machines and filmed at the rate of 2,000 to 2,500 per hour. About 1,600 letters could be filmed on one roll.

The switch to film made a major difference in the volume of mail that could be handled. It was estimated that 150,000 ordinary one-sheet letters would weigh 2,575 pounds and fill 37 mail sacks. At the same time, using 150,000 of the microfilmed sheets would save 2,530 pounds and the space for 36 additional sacks of mail.

The Post Office Department did not have control over the V-Mail stations. Instead it was responsible for separating mail according to the units for which it was destined.

Armed Forces personnel overseas got free use of the V-Mail simply by putting their name rank and unit in the space for the return address and writing "free" where the stamp would normally go.

The original V-Mail letters on film were not destroyed until it had been ascertained that the V-Mail letters reached their destination.

More than one billion V-Mail letters were sent and received from Armed Forces personnel overseas from June 1942 until November 1945 when the service was discontinued. V-Mail letters were thereafter sent in the original form until the supply of sheets was exhausted in March 1946.

In later years we would talk about nuclear missiles that made victory possible in a difficult war. But, to this day, many a veteran has a place in his or her memory album for the tiny V letter sheets that brought home and victory closer and sooner in World War II.

1914–1918

★WORLD★WAR★I★

World War I was truly a world war in the broadest sense of the name. Before the shooting stopped the war had seen the involvement of four Central Powers: Germany, Turkey, Austria-Hungary, and Bulgaria. Massed against them on the Allied side were Serbia, Belgium, France, the British Empire, Japan, Portugal, Montenegro, Italy, San Marino, Rumania, Greece, the United States, Brazil, Cuba, Panama, Haiti, Guatemala, Honduras, Costa Rica, Nicaragua, Liberia, China, and Siam. Additionally, Bolivia, Ecuador, Peru, and Uruguay broke off diplomatic relations with Germany.

The theoretical cause of World War I was the assassination of Archduke Francis Ferdinand and his wife of Austria-Hungary by Serbian agitators at Sarajevo in Bosnia in June of 1914. The more realistic cause was probably the political and economic rivalries of the major world powers as they sought to expand their domain and influence.

A month after the assassination, Austria-Hungary sent Serbia an ultimatum demanding punishment of those involved within 48 hours. When no satisfactory response was received, Austria-Hungary declared war on Serbia.

Events moved at a furious pace after that, with the map of Europe looking like a jigsaw puzzle that had been dumped from its box. So many countries became involved in the conflict that it was necessary to read the daily papers to find out which countries were fighting on a given day.

The United States did not enter the war until the last two years, declaring war on Germany on April 6, 1917. On December 7 — a date that was destined to live in infamy in the chronicle of a later war — the United States declared war on Austria-Hungary. The United States was involved in helping supply the Allies during the early years of the war, but it did not formally get into the conflict until the Germans began heavy use of submarines to cut the supply lines.

World War I introduced new weapons and new fighting techniques. The first of these was the development of trench warfare on a grand scale. Miles of these trenches stretched across the battlefield. Some were reinforced with wood or metal. Others were just ditches dug in the ground. Each contained hundreds of soldiers facing each other ready to do battle with the troops on the other side.

World War I also brought new war machines. Submarines slid under the water posing an ever-present threat of underwater demolition to troop and cargo ships. Tanks were developed from a design for tractors used in the United States before the war. Primitive aircraft were employed for observation and later for fighting and bombing missions.

World War I also extracted a heavy toll in human life. By the time the war ended in 1918 it had cost about 8.7 million lives including 120,000 Americans.

In August 1915, while preparing to move his family to quarters at Fort Bliss, El Paso, TX, Brig. Gen. John J. Pershing was informed that his wife and three little daughters, ages 8, 7 and 6, perished in a fire at the family's quarters at the Presidio in San Francisco. His son Francis Warren, 5, was rescued by a servant. In May 1916, one month after a state of war was declared with Germany, Gen. Pershing was named Commander-in-Chief of all American forces in Europe by President Woodrow Wilson. "Auntie May" was entrusted with Warren's care for the war's duration. Warren visited his father in France after the war and wore his French Marshal's uniform referred to in Gen. Pershing's letter.

When World War II began, Warren enlisted as a private, later attended Officer Candidate School, and became a major in an engineer battalion by the end of the war.

Gen. Pershing was buried in 1948 on a quiet knoll at Arlington National Cemetery. Beside him rests Warren's son, 2nd Lt. Richard Pershing, who died of wounds received in action in Vietnam in February 1968.

France, March 19, 1919

"My dear Warren:

"Don't you wish you had a stenographer to whom you could dictate your letters, so you would not have to write them? I guess you do wish so. At least I would think so from the way the bad pen and the bad pencil seem to work for you. Ink is not always good, is it? Funny how ink will spill off of pens and spoil letters. I remember when I was a little boy I used to be just the same way. It is not so easy to write, but then you know little boys must learn to do things well, even if it is a little hard to learn. And it is always better to learn when you are a little boy because it comes easier than when you grow up. There are lots of things I wish I had learned better when I was a little boy, as I might not have to work now.

"You know little boys' school days pass very quickly. They do not seem to pass very quickly, but the first thing you know they are gone, then you are a man and you cannot go to school any more because you have to work, and may be you have a lot of other things to think about and do not get much time to study and learn to write. I think if you wrote letters oftener it would soon come quite easy for you. Try it and see.

"The pictures of the little Field Marshal came to-day. They have been a long time on the road. I do not know what happened to them, but I suppose they have been piled under a lot of other mail somewhere and probably got lost for awhile. Anyway, I think they are very good.

"Auntie May wrote me about your putting on the uniform and wearing it to school. I think that was a very nice thing to do, because all the little boys and girls now know what a real Marshal of France looks like, and they did not know before. You cannot tell as

much by looking at pictures as you can from seeing a real Marshal in a real uniform. I expect they will remember that a long time.

"You know a boy who has a nice uniform like that, a nice sword and cap and everything ought to be very careful about riding his wheel and not take too many chances about running into street cars, and when he sees a street car coming (and he ought to be on the lookout for them all the time) he should stop until the street car passes by. How do you suppose I knew about your running so close to a street car? I wont tell you now. I will have to tell you some other time. Maybe you can guess, but you must be very careful, because I would like to think of you as being careful.

"You know it takes a long time for letters to reach me, and I think for that reason we must write each other more frequently than we do. I will write you as often as I have time, and you promise to write me as often as you have time. Of course I know little boys have to have a lot of time to play, and I want my little boy to have lots of time to play. I think he would get about as much out of play as he would writing letters, as a rule, but you know when anybody wants a letter from his little boy as much as I do, then may be he might take a little less time to play and a little more to write letters. Play is very necessary and I am glad you like to play, as I want you to be out of doors and grow big and strong.

"I hope you get well over the measles, and am glad you had them. You won't have to have them again, maybe.

"Good night, many kisses."

George W. Lee, Battery D, 317th Field Artillery, wrote to his mother in Greensboro, NC, from France on Nov. 11, 1917.

"Dear Mama,

"I am well and feeling good as I have just been to dinner, and had all I wanted to eat, and you know that is what pleases me. Just give me plenty to eat and I will take care of the rest.

"It is quite different here about buying things to eat. Candy is hard to get! no oranges or peaches at all; eggs about 15 francs a dozen. The people over here think we Americans are all millionaires, and we have to pay high for things.

"I wish I could see you all, I could tell you many things I am not allowed to write. All our letters are blue penciled. I am not allowed to tell you where I am, and whatever my duty is, that shall I do to the fullest extent.

"If you want to do something for us please, boost the Y.M.C.A., also the Red Cross. They are both wonderful organizations. The Y.M.C.A. is our only home and the Red Cross girls our mothers. Believe me, I can never do enough for them. If the folks at home do their share, we will sure do ours for you, and do it willingly.

"Gee! I often think of the time when I was at home. Mama you know I believe that one day I will come back to you and the loved ones I left behind. Wouldn't you be glad to have your soldier boy with you again? My prayer to God is that we will have peace with all the nations and we boys get back home with our dear ones."

F.G. Pence, U.S. Army rank unknown, whose duties involved working in the Water Analysis Laboratory in Paris during World War I, wrote to his brother Otto, in Bowmans, Shenandoah County, VA, on August 17, 1918.

"Dear Brother: This morning (Sunday) I saw the inside of the Great Notre Dame situated on the Seine. The fellow Soldier who was with me said, "Could anyone imagine a place like this?" He spoke my feelings exactly for I don't think anyone could imagine a place similar to the Notre Dame. In one of the air raids, the Germans dropped a bomb about 40 yards from it a few months ago. In March they dropped 4 bombs in one place about two city blocks away from it. Although I am not a Catholic yet I certainly would hate to see them destroy it for I am certain that another could not be built like that one.

"I have seen my first air raid last Thursday night. The Germans came over about 11:30, but they did not do much damage and only caused a few difficulties in the suburbs of the city. I was sound asleep when the alarm was given and waking up suddenly with those sirens blowing in such a manner gives one a creepy feeling. Although the raid did not come in our section we had to stay up till 1:30 a.m.

"Have you been attending the picnicks much this summer? You must have a good time for me too and tell the Girls I will be with them next year and tell them about my summer spent in France; and how the girls kiss always on the cheek. Some of these French customs get my goat sometimes, for instance when you meet one on the street, she shakes hands and if you only talk a few moments with her she will shake again when she leaves you. They are not afraid to discuss sex with you either, although in a nice way while an American girl would never think of doing such a thing, provided she is decent. Sincerely yours, F.G. Pence"

To Red Cross Nurse Mary L. Whitaker
Somewhere in France, Sept. 17, 1918

"We surely did miss you. The first night Capt. M refused to give "Mike" a hypo, saying that he was afraid the nurses had commenced something they couldn't finish. If he could only have staid with that poor boy one night! That same night we opened T Ward in order to accommodate the new influenza patients from the Aero squadron. Friday night Mike gave Jean a bad scare, the O.D., Lt. H. was called and wonder-of-wonders—he came at once. He and Capt. G tried to get some sort of response from the boy. Finally, he came to. A hypo relieved him for the rest of the night. That same night Hanselman in O Ward, the pneumonia patient, caused us considerable worry while Chappel surprised us by sleeping quietly almost all night. Lt. B. was consulted at midnight and later the O.D. at 2 o'clock. M. and O. were prescribed at both times, there being little else to do for him. Lt. H. was very nice about being called out of bed, especially when one considers how very cold it was that morning. His knees and hands shook so much that he could scarcely hold the spoon in his hands. One half hour after R and I went off duty the man expired. I thot I realized what your job was like, but I found out differently when your responsibilities were thrust upon my shoulders after you left....

"Now I didn't intend writing so much, but I dare not close without again expressing the pleasure and what a privilege it was for me to have made your acquaintance and associated with you during those six weeks spent at the hospital. Your cheerful and radiant personality was not only better than medicine for the patients who were fortunate enuf to come under your tender care, but your conscientiousness and interest in your work as well were an inspiration to the men who worked with you. As for the patients, Mike's remarks to Jean ought to be considered quite complimentary, for he remarked 'That Miss Whitaker is a fine woman; I could just kiss her for bein' so good to me.' And right here I might add that I fear Mike will not live many days, but I venture to prophesy that he'll die fighting to the last. As for the night men, I know I voice the sentiments of all when I say that our work was made a pleasure because of your presence. I am not given to flattering, and I don't want you to consider these remarks as such. I believe you have a right to know that your efforts have not been in vain, but produced some lasting results.

"And so as I leave for the Front to face the shot and shell of the enemy, I go unafraid, but with the hope and prayer that, should I be called upon to suffer as I have seen others suffer, I shall find a Red Cross nurse such as you, unless Providence should be so kind as to bring me under the care of the Original.

"My candle is almost burned out so I had better finish this letter anyway, it's almost time for taps. With best wishes I remain sincerely yours,

"Herbert C. Kimmel (Pvt..) Med. Det. 13th F.A."

Battery D Commander, Capt. Harry S Truman of the 35th Division, 129th Field Artillery, wrote frequently to his future bride, Bess Wallace, of Independence, MO. Excerpts from letters written from the front lines of France in World War I in 1918 follow:

"You know when I was a kid, say about thirteen or fourteen, I was a tremendous reader of heavy literature like Homer, Abbott's Lives, Leviticus, Isaiah and the memoirs of Napoleon. Then it was my ambition to make Napoleon look like a sucker and I thirsted for a West Point education so I could be one of the oppressors, as the kid said when asked why he wanted to go there. You'd never guess why I had such a wild desire and you'll laugh when I tell you. It was only so you could be the leading lady of the palace or empire or whatever it was I wanted to build. You may not believe it but my notion as to who is the best girl in the world has never changed and my military ambition has ended by having arrived at the post of centurion. That's a long way from Caesar, isn't it? Now I want to be a farmer. Can you beat it? I'm hoping you'll like the rube just as well as you would have Napoleon. I'm sure the farmer would be happier."

"Personally, I'd rather be a Battery commander than a brigadier general. I am virtually the dictator of the action of 194 men and if I succeed in making them work as one, keep them healthy morally and physically and make 'em write to the mamas and sweethearts, and bring 'em all home, I shall be nearly pleased with myself as I ever expect to be—until the one great event in my life is pulled off, which I am fondly hoping will take place immediately on my having delivered the 194 men in U.S.A. You'll have to take a leading part in that event you know and then for one great future."

At 4 p.m. on June 28, 1919, seven weeks after 35-year-old Capt. Truman was discharged at Camp Funston, and almost nine years after he began his courtship of Bess Wallace and six years since she accepted him, they were married at Trinity Church, a few blocks from 219 North Delaware Street, Independence, MO.

"Your welcomed letter of July 5 received and I was very glad to hear from you. I was also glad you received the card stating I arrived safely overseas. I suppose it made you feel better after the U-Boat scare.

"I cannot tell you what part of the country I am in, but I have seen a whole lot of it, and most of it was by walking.

"I have been up in the trenches. It was pretty quite while I was up there. When we were in the support they use to shell us. One day they kept sending shells over for about a half an hour and they were landing right around us. We were pretty lucky we didn't lose a man.

"We have had quite a little rain over here but it is better now. It rained every day for over a week. A soldier's life is allright in France as long as the weather stays clear but when it rains it is a rotten life. I hate to think of winter coming. It will be a cold job in the trenches, but we still have to take the bitter with the sweet.

"I have seen quite a few air fights. Some nights they fly over the towns all night, but don't seem to do much damage.

"I saw Gen. Pershing today he came around to inspect our division. He certainly is a fine looking man. He said the men were in good shape, and seemed to be pleased with us. I suppose he will have us shipped up to the front again. I only wish you could see the rats in the trenches. I believe they are as big as cats.

"We lost our last old officer Lieut. Jemson, they sent him back to the States for an instructor. But we still have a good set of officers.

"Well I guess I have told you all the censor will let me so I will close hoping this letter finds you all in the best of health. Tell mother I hope to get back soon and eat a good square meal with her. As ever, Geo."

Eighteen-year-old Pvt. George Barlow, Jr., Company E, 114th Infantry, was killed in action October 12 in the battle of the Argonne, two months after he wrote this letter to his father in Trenton, NJ.

1898–1899

SPANISH AMERICAN WAR

The Spanish American War was at least partially the result of a much smaller war a circulation war —between two New York newspaper giants.

Joseph Pulitzer, owner of The New York World, and William Randolph Hearst, owner of The New York Journal, made their newspapers look like some present day scandal tabloids as they battled to sell more newspapers.

In Cuba rebels were fighting to free their country from Spain. The newspapers in New York played up every skirmish and emblazoned it with tales of atrocities, murder, and even romance. They were practicing a kind of super-patriotism known as "jingoism."

American business interests added to the fire as they sought to exploit the trade and resources up for grabs in Cuba.

The war fever reached a new height in February 1898 when the Battleship Maine was blown up while on a visit to Havana Harbor. The tragedy took 260 American lives. While no responsibility was fixed for the explosion, the New York papers put the blame solely on Spain and urged immediate retaliation. "Remember the Maine" became a rallying cry to bring the United States into the war. Congress went along and war was declared within two months. Spain declared war on the United States on April 24.

Theodore Roosevelt, an Undersecretary of the Navy, began preparation for the battle. On February 25, when he was acting Secretary, he ordered Commodore (later admiral) George Dewey to see that the Spanish fleet did not leave the Philippines if the United States and Spain went to war.

Roosevelt left his Navy post and was commissioned a lieutenant colonel. He also received permission to organize a cavalry regiment to fight in Cuba. Both the commander and the troops he recruited seemed a most unlikely force. He called the group the "Rough Riders," and they were properly named. They included cowboys from the west, dandies from the east, and an assortment of gamblers, former convicts, and other outcasts. They were poorly outfitted and lacked training. All they had going for them was an intense desire to get into battle.

By the time Roosevelt got them to Cuba they seemed to be even less "combat ready." The Army had no summer uniforms to issue them so they wore heavy winter outfits in the Cuban heat. They also became separated from their horses shortly after they got ashore. Nevertheless, Roosevelt led them in his famous charge up what was incorrectly called San Juan Hill. Its correct name was Kettle Hill.

While the Rough Riders were fighting in Cuba, Admiral Dewey won a seven-hour battle against the Spanish Navy in Manila Harbor, effectively ending the war.

Under terms of the Spanish surrender the U.S. was given Guam and Puerto Rico and agreed to pay Spain $20 million for the Philippines. Cuba was placed under U.S. control for three years.

OLYMPIA

sa Walker, Commander of the USS Concord, wrote to his son on May 4, 1898, to describe the American victory against the Spanish fleet in the battle of Manila Bay.

"You may fire when ready, Gridley," ordered Adm. George Dewey from the flagship "Olympia" of the Americans' Asiatic Squadron early in the morning of May 1, 1898. Steaming single file into Manila Bay and with guns blazing, the squadron totally vanquished the Spanish fleet without losing a single seaman.

"My Dear Boy: I have been so busy for the last four days that they seem a life time. Even now, I can scarcely believe that the events which have taken place are true. To begin, we sailed from Mirs Bay on the afternoon of April 26 — and steered for Cape Bolanan on the coast of the island of Luzon, about a hundred and thirty miles from Manilla. At about 5 o'clock on the morning of April 30th the Concord was signalled to proceed with the Boston to investigate Subic Bay, and find out if there were any vessels there. We entered the Bay just after noon, and made a thorough inspection of the bay finding nothing. Coming out we rejoined the fleet and took our position. The commanding officers went on board the flagship and received the last verbal orders for the coming engagement. The fleet steamed slowly down the coast for the entrance to Manilla Bay, distant about thirty five miles. At a little after twelve we saw a small island, el Fraile, which was to be the turning point, the fleet being in column of vessels, in the following order, which was kept throughout; Olympia, Baltimore, Raleigh, Petrel, Concord, Boston. Four of the ships turned without any apparent notice from those occupying the island, and just as the Concord put her helm over to swing into the new course, a rocket was sent up, and shortly afterward a shot whipped by evidently aimed at the stern light of the vessel ahead of her. I immediately ordered the fire returned, but owing to the failure of the primer, the Raleigh got in a shot before I could do so. However I sent in two shortly thereafter in reply to two others from the foe.

"One of our shots exploded directly over the battery and from their silence thereafter we concluded that they were frightened. The Boston and three auxilliaries passed unmolested. We stood on very slowly up the bay toward the town, the men sleeping at the guns, ready at a second's notice to spring to their work. At about four o'clock I served out hot coffee and food to the crew so that they might not fight hungry.

"In the early dawn as the shipping and houses at Manilla began to show up, the flagship made the signal, "Follow the motions of the flagship," and then headed for the city, to pass at about two thousand yards, the shallow water not permitting a nearer approach. We had been told that the two heaviest Spanish vessels were anchored close in shore at the end of the breakwater, and we intended to silence them as we passed, but they were not there and we passed on. In passing a battery opened on us from the city front, I replied to it with one of our six-inch guns and have since learned that the shot struck within a dozen feet of the gun. Slowly we swept down toward Kavete where the Spanish fleet had concentrated and which was armed with heavy shore batteries, and whose approaches were mined. The mines were exploded before we were anywhere near them, and the ships and batteries opened when we were miles away. All was silent within our fleet until the Olympia got within about three thousand yards, and then she opened with her whole battery, shortly after the Baltimore chipped in, followed by each vessel in succession as the guns bore and soon we were hammering away for all we were worth. The fleet passed on, turned and again and once again went over the same path, throwing in a most infernal fire. At 7:40 we passed out of action to take breakfast the first gun having been fired at five minutes past five. You can have no idea of the scene. The old expression "Hell broke loose" was perfectly exemplified—I have written more fully to Belle and asked her to send you a copy of what I have written to her.

"When we hauled out of action we could not estimate what damage we had done though we saw ships in flames and others sinking. In a little while, however, we saw flames issuing from other vessels and realized that the whole thing was with us— There were six minor casualties on board the Baltimore. These were all that were hurt in the Squadron. Four ships were hit but not injured. The Petrel and Concord were untouched.

"We have destroyed the whole Spanish fleet. Two cruisers, nine gunboats of size from twelve hundred tons down and two transports. We have taken numerous tugs and launches, and expect to take some more tomorrow—We have destroyed five batteries to my knowledge, and how many more I don't know—we have received the surrender of the Naval Arsenal, and the military there, and have put a force on shore there. Kavete is a little place that we can keep easily and police —Manilla we have not touched as we do not care to have it on hand to keep in order —We possess the bay and have the power to enforce a strict blockade —It has been hard work, sleepless nights and days without rest — tomorrow will be another busy day.

"The effect of our fire on the Spanish ships is said to have been something terrific. There were hundreds killed and many more wounded—The Comd'r in Chief has expressed himself as having been faithfully sustained by his Commanding Officers. Where each one did his duty there can be no distinction drawn. When I get more time, dear boy, I shall write more fully to you. I haven't recovered from my excessive fatigue of forty hours on the bridge. I forgot to say that after our breakfast following the fight, we got underway and shelled the batteries and Arsenal, and later it fell to me to burn the large mail steamer La Isla de Mindanao. Wasn't all this fine Sunday work? Wasn't it wonderful that we lost not a man? And are you not glad that the 'old man' didn't funk? Well, goodbye, my boy! Study hard to learn how to save life instead of how to take it. God bless and keep you! Pardon the pencil. Ever your loving father, Asa Walker."

U.S. MAIL
3.A
HEAD BROS PHOTO.
THE EMPLOYEES OF THE R.M.S. P.O. AT CHICAMAUGA POSTAL STATION 6-26-98
AND REGIMENTAL MAIL CARRIERS U.S.A.

"Yesterday we struck the Spaniards and had a brisk fight for two and a half hours before we drove them out of their position. We lost a dozen men killed or mortally wounded, and sixty severely or slightly wounded....One man was killed as he stood beside a tree with me. Another bullet went through a tree behind which I stood, and filled my eyes with bark. The last charge I led on the left using a rifle I took from a wounded man; and I kept three of the empty cartridges we got from a dead Spaniard...for the children. Every man behaved well; there was no flinching. The fire was very hot at one or two points where the men around me went down like ninepins....

"I have been sleeping on the ground in the mackintosh, and so drenched with sweat that I haven't been dry a minute day or night....My bag has never turned up, like most of our baggage...I have nothing with me, no soap, toothbrush, razor, brandy, medicine chest, socks, or underclothes...

"For four days I never took off my clothes...and we had no chance to boil the water we drank...The morning after the fight we buried our dead in a great big trench, reading the solemn burial services over them, and all the regiment joining in singing 'Rock of Ages.' The vultures were wheeling overhead by hundreds. They plucked out the eyes and tore the faces and wounds of the dead Spaniards before we got to them, and even one of our own men who lay in the open. The wounded lay in the path, a ghastly group; but there were no supplies for them...the woods are full of land crabs...when things grew quiet they slowly gathered in gruesome rings around the fallen."

Theodore Roosevelt resigned his position as Assistant Secretary of the Navy to accept a commission as Lieutenant Colonel with the First U.S. Volunteer Cavalry, known popularly as the "Rough Riders." He wrote to his wife after leading his men against the Spanish forces in Cuba in June 1898.

ROUGH RIDERS
3¢
US POSTAGE
1898
1948

Charles Remington, an enlisted man serving with Company D of the 3rd Wisconsin, wrote to his family in Mauston, WI from Coamo, Puerto Rico, on September 22, 1898. Dan was his older brother.

"...While on guard a couple of natives came along that wanted to sell me something in a sack. I motioned to open the sack and they showed me a Spanish sergent uniform. It was new and never had been put on. I bought it for $2 in American money and they went off satisfied and so was I. I have been offered $4 already. It is made of light blue material with small white stripes. It is well made with green trimings and gold braid chevrons. On the collar there are two no. 10 that indicates the regiment. I think it is quite a bargain and it fits Dan to perfection....We expect mail this evening and I hope it comes for it has been a week since we received any. I guess you folk will think that I am not writing much but a well man gets guard every other day and plenty of other details between times."

little leisure now, We have moved our
quarters from near New Manila, to the
Arsenal called Fort Santaigo with
walled city. They have tons of all
projectiles and cannon balls stac
inside the Fort, the walls of whi
about 25 or … and 5
high, and see … from
passing throug … numb
prisoners kep … on helping to
bandage som … ded today.
I sent you … my photos.
yesterday, so … ll recieve them
when you get this.

"I suppose by the time you get this the wintry winds will be sweeping over Pennsylvania, and the buckwheat cakes and sausage will be ripe.

"As Uncle Sam does not issue buckwheat flour and make sausages, we don't get any, but we do get bread with nice plump red ants in it and you know I was always a great boy for ants. The coffee is liken unto that which our mothers used to make, that is when they made it out of roasted boot legs and dish water.

"We have beef steak sometimes— have you ever eaten a nice juicy piece of India rubber you would certainly prefer it to our beef."

William S. Christner, of the 10th Pennsylvania, wrote to his mother and father from Manila on October 17, 1898.

Theodore Hardnacke of the 12th U.S. Infantry Hospital Corps wrote to his family on March 3, 1899, en route to Manila.

"Dearest folks at home, it is once on my long voyage that I have had a oppertunity to write, and I am glad I have the pleasure to do so. We left the Brooklyn navy yards at 3:30 p.m Sunday, Feb. 18. I am in the best of health and have been since I left you. the sea has been very calm, I am injoying the trip, and think it is the trip of my life, I had a nice trip to North Brothers Island, New York the day we left. It was 15 miles from were the Transport was, I had four sick men to take there witch could not go to Manila. I went on a little government tug. I went under the Brooklyn Bridge and had a full view of New York.

"Well we made Gibraltar this morning and it is a lovely place, there is North Africa on one side and Spain on the other, Gibraltar belonks to England, it is a English Fortification.

"Well Mary we will make 5 stops before we get to Manila, and I will wright you a letter at every place we stop. I have not been sea sick yet but there has been a good many that has, There has been only one died, and he was buried at sea. Dr. L. C. Malwee send me a fine Medical Dictionary, and he told me how to take care of myselfe. I follied his instructions, and I guess that is the reason I have not been sick.

"Well Mary how are all of you at home, send all the folk my regards and I wish you were here now, the lights are all burning bright, and it is butiful, one of bands are playing, the stars and stripes for ever, Well Mary do not laugh at my righting for I will try to do better the next time so good by. Love to all from your brother Theodore."

Company E, 10th Regulars PA Vols.

Let us read old letters awhile,
Let us try to hear
The thin, forgotten voices of men forgotten
Crying out of torn scraps of paper, notes scribbled and smudged
On aces, on envelope-backs, on gilt-edged cards stolen
out of a dead man's haversack.

Other voices, arising out of the scraps of paper,
Till they mix in a single voice that says over and over
"It is cold. It is wet. We marched till we couldn't stand up.
It is muddy here. I wish you could see us here.
They would know what war is like. We are still patriotic.
We are going to fight. We hope this general's good.
We hope he can make us win. We'll do all we can.
But I wish we could show everybody who stays at home
What this is like."
Voices of tired men,
Sick, convalescent, afraid of being sick.

Excerpts from
JOHN BROWN'S BODY
Steven Vincent Benet

☆ THE ☆ CIVIL ☆ WAR ☆

The Civil War was perhaps the most misnamed war in the history of the United States. It was anything but civil.

It was mean, dirty, and vicious. It pitted families against families, brothers against brothers, and even fathers against sons. It was fought not like conventional wars with trained forces meeting each other on the field of combat. Instead it took young farm boys, poorly equipped and even more poorly trained, and sent them out to do battle with some of their former friends and neighbors.

Most of the wars in which the United States was involved found a united country fighting against a common enemy. This war found a country torn apart by economic and political realities. The tear was deep and the scars lasted a long time after the war ended.

Economic matters were among the major causes. The South was an agrarian economy and enjoyed the growth and prosperity harvested from its fields. By contrast, the North was moving rapidly into the age of the industrial revolution. Inventions such as the cotton gin made it possible for the factories of the North to process cotton much faster. To take advantage of this productivity, the North needed more and more cotton from the South. To meet this demand the South had to have abundant cheap labor. They felt this meant they needed the right to buy and keep slaves to work the fields.

Who would prevail? The issue was not to be resolved in any courtroom. States fought for the right to control their own destiny. The national leadership fought to form a strong union between North and South in which both would prosper.

The South believed the only solution was to leave the Union and form its own nation. South Carolina seceded in December of 1860. Mississippi, Florida, Alabama, Georgia, Louisiana and Texas followed. They formed the Confederate States of America and named Jefferson Davis as their president. The war began when the Confederates fired on Fort Sumter in April of 1861. President Lincoln called for troops to be used against seceding states. Two days later Virginia seceded followed by Arkansas, North Carolina, and Tennessee. Kentucky and Missouri did not secede, but they sent representatives to the Confederate Congress.

The war ended in 1865 after a series of routs by the Yankee forces. General Sheridan defeated the Confederates at Five Forks. The Confederates evacuated Richmond and General Robert E. Lee surrendered to Grant at Appomattox.

The Merrimac, at left, with guns blazing, rams the Monitor.

The young and inexperienced Lt. Samuel Dana Greene, Executive Officer, U.S. Steamer Monitor, Hampton Roads, VA, March 14, 1862, wrote to his family of the fight between the Union's Monitor and the C.S.S. Virginia — a ship originally called the "Merrimack" before she was scuttled, raised, rebuilt, and refitted with protective iron sheathes by the Confederacy. The first sea battle between two clumsy, barely seaworthy iron-clad ships would profoundly affect future naval warfare, and show that wooden ships could not prevail in battle against them. Although Greene claimed victory for the Monitor, more experienced persons viewed the outcome a standoff, with just a slight "edge" for the Monitor.

The letters in this section reflect the mixed emotions soldiers felt as they matched family loyalty against the needs of the country. The letters show the bitterness felt in the heat of battle. They also show the empathy as both sides briefly halted the war to bury their dead..a kind of silent truce..and then the battle resumed.

"At daylight we discovered the Merrimac at anchor with several vessels under Sewell's Point. We immediately made every preparation for battle. At 8 a.m. on Sunday the Merrimac got underweigh accompanied by several steamers and steered direct for the Minnesota. When a mile distant she fired two guns at the Minnesota. By this time our anchor was up, the men at quarters, the guns loaded, and everything ready for action. As the Merrimac came closer the Captain passed the word to commence firing. I triced up the port ran the gun out and fired the first gun and thus commenced the great battle between the Monitor and the Merrimac.

"Now mark the condition our men were in. Since Friday morning, 40 hours, they had had no rest, and very little food, as we could not conveniently cook. They had been hard at work all night, had nothing to eat for breakfast except hard bread, and were throroughly worn out. As for myself, I had not slept a wink for 51 hours, and had been on my feet almost constantly. But after the first gun was fired we forgot all fatigue, hard work and everything else, and went to work fighting as hard as men ever fought.

"We loaded and fired as fast as we could. The shot, shell, grape, canister, musket, and rifle balls flew in every direction, but did us no damage. Our tower was struck several times, and though the noise was pretty loud it did not affect us any. At about 11:30 the Captain sent for me.

"I went forward, and there stood as noble a man as lives at the foot of the ladder of the Pilot House. His face was

perfectly black with powder and iron and he was apparently perfectly blind. I asked him what was the matter. He said a shot had struck the Pilot House and blinded him. He told me to take charge of the ship and use my own discretion. I led him to his room and laid him on the sofa and then took his position. We still continued firing, the tower being under the direction of Stimers. We were now between two fires, the Minnesota on one side, and the Merrimac on the other. The latter was retreating to Sewell's Point.

"The fight was over now and we were victorious. My men and myself were perfectly black, and my person in the same condition.

"When our noble Captain heard the Merrimac had retreated he said he was happy and willing to die since he had saved the Minnesota. Ah! how I love to venerate that man, most fortunately for him his classmate and most intimate friend Lieut. Wise saw the fight and was alongside immediately after the engagement. He took him on board the Baltimore boat and carried him to Washington.

"The next morning we got under weigh at 8 and stood through our fleet. Cheer after cheer went up from frigates and small craft for the glorious little Monitor and happy inded did we all feel. I was Captain then of the vessel that had saved Newport News, Hampden Roads, Fortress Monroe (as General Wool himself said) and perhaps your Northern Ports.

"Batsy, my old room-mate was on board the 'Merrimac'. Little did we ever think at the Academy we should be firing 150 lb balls at each other. But so goes the world."

Just appointed his unit's adjutant, John Singleton Mosby's life as a private soldier was over. He had to begin to dress like an officer and he needed the help of his wife, Pauline. This promotion indeed would be a stepping stone for Mosby, who would become a trusted aide to cavalry Gen. J.E.B. Stuart. By war's end, Mosby would become arguably the best known and most feared guerilla in the Confederacy, leading the 43rd Virginia (Partisan) Battalion, "Mosby's Rangers."

Camp lst Virginia Cavalry
February 14th, 1862

My Dearest Pauline,

...I want you to go up to Lynchburg and get me a neat uniform. Crenshaw's clothes are the best. You could buy the cloth home. All I want is something neat but nothing fine. Get me a pair of shoulder straps and a blue cap I prefer. I will send you a letter Sunday with some money. ... Please send my clothes as quickly as possible as I have nothing decent to wear and my present position requires that I should. Send them by Express and take a receipt and enclose to me. Also some socks.

When I was a private I could not go off without leave but now that I am an officer I have more privileges. I would not desire you to come just now as you would have to stay six or seven miles from camp and the roads are in such a condition that you would be almost as far off as now. Love to all kiss my babes for me.

Yours affectionately,
Jno. S. Mosby

Colonel John S. Mosby is seated in the middle with some of his rangers.

Washington D.C.
May 25. 1861

To the Father and Mother of Col.
Elmer E. Ellsworth:

My dear Sir and Madam,

In the untimely loss of your noble son, our affliction here, is scarcely less than your own. So much of promised usefulness to one's country, and of bright hopes for one's self and friends, have rarely been so suddenly dashed, as in his fall. In size, in years, and in youthful appearance, a boy only, his power to command men, was surpassingly great. This power, combined with a fine intellect, an indomitable energy, and a taste altogether military, constituted in him, as seemed to me, the best natural talent, in that department, I ever knew.

And yet he was singularly modest and deferential in social intercourse. My acquaintance with him began less than two years ago; yet through the latter half of the intervening period, it was as intimate as the disparity of our ages, and my engrossing engagements, would permit. To me, he appeared to have no indulgences or pastimes; and I never heard him utter a profane, or an intemperate word. What was conclusive of his good heart, he never forgot his parents. The honors he labored for so laudably, and, in the sad end, so gallantly gave his life, he meant for them, no less than for himself.

In the hope that it may be no intrusion upon the sacredness of your sorrow, I have ventured

to address you this tribute to the
memory of my young friend, and
your brave and early fallen child.
May God give you that consolation which is beyond all earthly
power—

Sincerely your friend
in a common af-
fliction—
A. Lincoln

On May 24, 1861, the morning after Virginia announced secession from the Union, a large Confederate flag flew over the Marshall House in Alexandria, Virginia, placed there by hotel manager James Jackson, who vowed allegiance to the South. Col. Ellsworth, after landing at Alexandria with a Union occupying force, hauled down the flag from the roof, and was shot as he descended the stairs by Jackson, who was also killed by one of Ellsworth's soldiers, Cpl. Francis Brownell. The two slain men would be honored as martyrs to their causes. President Lincoln wrote to the parents of the young colonel he once called "the greatest little man I ever met," on May 25, 1861, to express his sorrow for his death. The funeral of the 24-year-old Zouave leader — the first officer to die in the conflict — was held in the East Room of the White House.

"Having distributed such poor Christmas gifts as I have to those around me, I have been looking for something for you. Trifles are hard to get these war times, and you must not therefore expect more. I have sent you what I thought more useful...and hope it (a gift of money) will be of some service...

"I send you some sweet violets that I gathered for you this morning while covered with dense white frost, whose crystals glittered in the bright sun like diamonds and formed a brooch of rare beauty and sweetness which could not be fabricated by the expenditure of a world of money. May God guard and preserve you for me, my dear daughter! Among the calamities of war, the hardest to bear, perhaps, is the separation of families and friends...In my absence from you I have thought of you very often, and regretted I could do nothing for your comfort..."

Gen. Robert E. Lee wrote a Christmas letter from camp in December 1861, the first Christmas of the war, to one of his daughters.

"The whole army is on the move again and I think we will cross the river soon. The rebel pickets and ours trade papers every day and our boys swap coffee for wiskey with them. The 24th Wis is at Bridgeport and that is where the bridge crosses the Tennessee River. The Rebels guard one end and the 24th boys the other. When they first went there the rebels shot at them all the while, but they have agreed not to shoot at one another until we try to cross in force."

George F. Alverson, of the 24th Wisconsin, Anderson Station, wrote to his father, William, Heart Prairie, Walworth County, WI, on August 15, 1862.

July 30, 1862

To Mrs. Fannie A. Cater
Burnt Corn, Belleville, Conecuh Co, Alabama

Dear Cousin Fannie,

The long, sultry summer days come and go, weeks lapse into months and months glide away, yet no little white-winged messenger comes to cheer the lonely hours or tell me of the absence of loved ones.

I never hear from home now. Home! Is there not magic in the word, poetry in the sound? Home—where my happy childhood dwelt, where joys, since unknown, nestled beneath the paternal roofs, where affection was riveted with a confidence unshaken. Are not its inmates dear as ever to me. Is not their welfare intimately interwoven with every fibril of my heart. The accursed invader has destroyed the ferry boats at Vicksburg and at Natchez and we must wait and wait in prolonged, painful suspense till accident, or till the termination of the war shall enable us to get any tidings from home.

Cousin Fannie if you should suspect that I am not passionately fond of soldier life I must acknowledge that the surmise is correct. But you must not think that the fire of patriotism burns with feebler flame in my bosom. The troubles of my country render her dear to me. Nor must you think that I would exchange the hardships or privations of camp life for the ease and comforts of home in this the hour of danger.

There is much in camp to disgust me; its hardships, its trials are not "trifles light as air," its dangers are not imagined and being real are not delights, for life is sweet; but while my health permits, I will endure all, till the goal is reached—till the crowning victory is won, till the star of the Confederacy is in the ascendency, shining pure and bright in the political constellation—in the national galaxy.

Rufus W. Cater
Co. E, 19th Regt. La. Vols
2nd Brigade Jones' Division Mobile, Ala

Rufus W. Cater was killed in action at Chickamauga.

Union soldier Nels Nelson wrote this letter in Swedish to his sister, Julia Nelson, on April 10, 1862, from Shiloh, Pittsburg Landing, TN.

"I will write a few lines about the big battle we have had here.

"There are many soldiers here and the camp is big. The regiment is camped very close to the south boundary.... The enemy came from the south on Sunday morning 6-7 a.m. just as we were having our breakfast. Then we were ordered to fall in line as fast as we could, which we did. Just as we came quickly as we could out of our tents, the cannon balls started flying over our heads. The tree tops and branches fell over the right flank of our company wounding one of our boys, before we had any chance to stand up against the enemy.

"At this time came far more cannons firing on us. We started to fire on them: on our side against the enemy before in full view. It was the best we could do. There fell Karl Sammuelson, then a few more. Sven Olson from Knoxville. They were shot in the head and killed. Then we must retreat, but stayed close to our cannons.

"The Rebels came from all sides; then we had to leave the cannons and we had to run as fast as we could so we would not be taken prisoners.

"Then we took persons of artillery and the horses and fled to the woods. The cannons we left got into enemy hands.

"After we ran awhile, we stopped to fight. The enemy rearranged their cannons firing on us again, but we stood our ground as long as it was possible. Comrades fell left and right very fast.

"Louis Berglaf, captain of our company was shot in the head. He came from Andover. The whole regiment was badly shot up. The Commander of the Regiment was injured also. We were once again surrounded and compelled to fall back and ran a half mile before we could turn around and stop them again.

"Then the Rebels plundered our camp to get our food, shoes and supplies. We turned the rebels around, pushed the enemy back again, but then our regiment was out of ammunition. Firing started and we fell back again at 3 P.M.

"We had a few "crackers" to eat to get some strength back again and back to battle 4 -5 P.M. The Rebels did not advance again. That night it was quiet and we got some rest and we were ready at daylight to meet the South again.

"We were soaked in the rain. It was hard for us, but we had to wait until the next morning. Then we walked forward. We met the enemy again with both cannons and rifles. We had a real battle that morning. It shook the ground. We fell back again. The enemy began to fall back and we got our camp back.

"As many as 200 from our Regiment were killed or injured...the Rebels captured many prisoners from us and we captured some of them.

"... Should I be called by God to ascend to heaven with my comrades, I hope you do not mourn for me. Written in haste,

Nels"

Murphreesboro, Tenn.
May 1, 1863

Dear Mary Jane,

We got to camp on the 30th of April we had a pretty good time... while we was out our Division took about 2 hundred rebels prisoner and a large number of horses besides a large abundance of forage and som flour. We burnt 3 rebel grist mills while we was out...when we started to go to a place called McMinnville but the mounted infantry and cavalry that was along with us started ahead of us the second day....there was considerable of a rebel force there but they did not make a stand...our men dashed in on them and they just got up in a rush and run...our men captured 150 of the cuses and also captured a train of cars between McMinnville and Manchester...we burnt the train...it was loaded with supplies for the rebels and our men also burnt several bridges on the Rail Road so that will be a hard strike on them in that part of the country...the fourth day that we was out we came to a rebel camp where they had to take there flight. They had to leve so sudent that they had not time to take there tents or camp equipment...they set a good many of there tents and wagons on fier so as we could make no use of them...our mounted men went out in the woods on the hunt for them...they found several of the scamps and we also got a part of the train that they had succeeded in getting away and our men found six pecies of artillery that they had hid out in the hills.

We brought in with us 19 rebels...I helpt to guard them day and night. I can tell you they don't like the idea of marching under the old Stars and Strips but they think that there families will have to starve for they say that the yankeys take all there corn and then burn there mills. They say there is no mill left within twenty miles of them....they say that the poor folks are just as well off as the rich...they say the poor folks has got no corn and the rich cannot get there corn ground. So you can see that they are begining to fear a dreadful end....

Write soon and often for if I do not get a letter from you ever week I think it is an awful long while....tell something about everything. I will quit for this time but write soon and often. From your affectionate husband, Isaac.

Isaac P.C. Raub

Letha Williams, from Blount County, AL, wrote on April 3, 1863, to her husband James, serving in the Confederate Army at Tullahoma, TN. James was killed in action. Her picture, taken several years later, shows the strength, courage and resourcefulness of women who "cope" while their men are at war.

"Very Deare companion it is threw the merses of God that I am permited to drop you a fiew lines to let you know that me & baby is boath as well & harty as we was when you left home & I truly hope that when these fiew lines comes to hand that they may find you enjoying the same great blesings of God.

"I hant got mutch to communicate to you as I have just rote to you but I have just red the letters you rote to me & your pap they gave me great satisfaction to read aline from you they maid five letters I have got from you & this is three I have rote to you & I dont know hardly how to rite without I knowed whether you got them or not   I will talk to you anyway but it ant because I dont love you James you dont know how bad I want to see you & talk with you & tell you about my loansome times here by ourselves I would give every thing I have got & more two if I had it if you was here this knight. but if I never see you again in this world I hope we will meet in heaven where parting of friend will be no more.

"I think of you so mutch that there is no use of talking about it & sometimes I think that if you never would come back I would give up & quit but then again I pick up heart & go to work & think that it wont do to not tri to do nothing for the will of God will be done enyhow.

"You wanted to know if i could read your bad riting I can read it as well as I wan to & don't neglect riting thinking I cant read it.... I got the stamps & money you sent me & I have sent you a ring maid of some of my hare & I want you to rite wheter you get it or not I will send you a lock of Marions in this letter I want you to send me your likeness if it costs you ten dollars. you can send it by male if you dont have no other chance Mr. Williams.

"I have got Miss Nations critter to plow & I have plowed and fixed large gober patch & has got a little corn planted & has planted beens & water melons.

"I want you to get a furlow & come home when you think they are ripe & help eat theme. you dont know how tired I am this knight a plowing & planting my things but I want to make enough to winter my cows for it can't be bought against & other winter.   Your paps folks & my paps folks is boath well I have got milk & butter & bread & meet to do me I have rote all this letter since supper & havt got up very time but my middle finger on my rite hand has got such a rising on it I cant rite anymore so I must close for I am tired & sleepy & loansome because you arnt here with me but I prey you may be sometime

"I still remain as your loving & affectionite wife until death

"(this is my true love hart & hand)

Letha Williams"

Lorenzo Vanderhoef wrote in his diary on May 19, 1863:

"What a pleasing [thing] it is to receive letters from our friends, and how glad I am that I took the advice of friends and practiced lettter writing when a small boy. By so doing I formed a habit, or rather a desire to read and write which now affords me many hours of real pleasure. During this war while so many of our dearest friends are away on the tented field, what hours and weeks of dreadful anxiety we would be obliged to endure were it not that we have a medium for communicating with them when distance separates us. How unpleasant must be the situation of those boys in our armies, who are unable to write to their friends and read letters received from them."

Tenth Ohioan Lorenzo *Vanderhoef* was wounded in September 1862 during one of the bloodiest battles of the Civil War — Antietam at Sharpsburg, MD. Vanderhoef's journal entry notes the value letters from friends and family play for him, and conversely the loss that fellow soldiers must experience who can neither read nor write.

The 8th Ohio had 341 men present for duty of 17 September at Sharpsburg, MD. Of these, 32 were killed and 129 were wounded when the battle commonly known as Antietam, was over.

Reuben C. Webb, 13th Illinois Cavalry, 7th Army, wrote from Little Rock, AR, on May 14, 1864, to his friend Mary Sealey in Detroit, MI. At that time there was no city delivery of mail and customers had to go to the post office to pick it up.

"Being that I have a little leisure time, I thought I would answer your kind and affectionate letter which I received this morning. I am well, happy and as Comfortable as can be expected for a Soldier. This Army Corps has just returned from a expidition which went to Cooperate with the Troops that moved up Red River under command of General Banks, our Troops here was under command of General Steel[e}; We left this place April 23rd and after Marching and Fighting about 6 weeks We returned to this place for a rest and not before we needed one.

"I will mention a few of the largest fights we had so you can see the account of them in the Papers. The first one was Terrenorris [Terre Noir] April 2nd, 64. The second one was Elkins Ferry April 4th 64. The Third one was Prarie DeAnne [Prairie D'Ane] April 10th 64. The Fourth one was Jenkins Ferry April 30th 64. Our loss in the expidition: about 3000 Killed Wounded and Missing. The last Battle was a heavy one. We had a small Band of 5000 men engaged, against 18 Thousand of the enemy. And against our Brave Boys, the Rebel General Kirby Smith, Hirled his force, but they were handsomely repulsed each time.

"Our boys were out of Aminittion when they made the last Charge. The boys lay low till they Came Close and then rushed on them and drove them at the Point of the Bayonet; our loss about 1 Hundred. A Citizen came in and reported the rebel loss 6 Thousand. We had 2 Negro Regiments in the late engagements. They made a dashing Charge at Jenkins Ferry and Captured 2 Piece of Artillary. The rebels did not like to have their Artillary taken by negroes! We had a Nice Artillary Duel at Liberty Station The Rebels had 8 Pieces and we had 6 The Duel lasted 1 hour and a half. In which time our Six Pieces threw 558 Shell. We silenced the Rebel Guns 7 times. We lost 2 Killed and 9 Wounded, by the explosion of Rebel Shells. Rebel loss not known. I am Dispatch Orderly for Brigadeier General S.A. Rice. He is laying at a Private Dwelling in the Place on account of a Wound which he received in our last engagement. He was shot by a Musket Ball in the right foot, Shooting the Spur Buckle in his foot which was not taken out for 5 days after he received the wound. The Doctor told me today that he was afraid he would loose his foot. He is a gallant officer and well liked by his men. Colonel Solomon, of the 9th Wisconsin Infantry is Commanding this Brigade, and so I have to Stay with him till the General Gets well. I hope he will soon get well for he was such a good man.

"You wished to know in your letter if I had reinlistred, I have not. General Steel said there was such a few of us and he could not give us furloughs, so we would not reinlist, if they would give me 30 Days Furlough to go home and see my friends, I think I would a tried 3 more years. My Time will be out in about 4 Months, but I think we Shant get to come home before Next Spring. When we came out we had 11 hundred men but now we have only 145 left and 30 of those are New recruits. Our regiment is about used up."

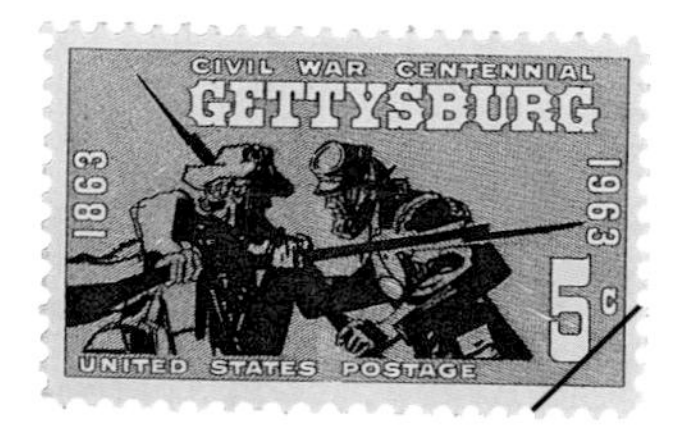

On August 1, 1866, from Augusta, ME, Union soldier LaGrange Severance wrote to William H. Rodgers of Brooks County, GA, about his encounter with Rodgers' son, a dying Confederate soldier.

"My dear Sir, I will now do a duty which I have been prevented from doing before on account of a want of mail facilities.

"I have been a soldier in the Federal Army: was at the battle of Cedar Creek, VA on the 19th of October, 1864, just at night of this day as we were advancing over ground lately gained. I came upon a soldier in gray uniform whose intelligent and expressive countenance so attracted my attention I could not resist the temptation to stop and learn something of him.

"He was a sergeant in Co. 'G' (I think), 26th Georgia regiment, and his name was Rodgers, but the first name I have forgotten. He was wounded in his left breast, and seemed conscious that he had but a short time to live. He told me he had a brother (older I think) lying dead but a few rods away. He was calm, quiet, and resigned, and said he would feel no anger for those who had caused his wound, as they, like himself, felt they were doing their duty. He seemed as quiet as though sleeping, suffering no pain. I gave him a drink of water, placed his blanket comfortably under his head, and pinned his name, regiment, and company upon it.

"In answer to my inquiry whether he wished any word sent any friend or relative, if ever opportunity offered, he said, 'If ever the war is over, and you can, write my father who lives in Quitman, Georgia and tell him where I died.' He then gave me your address.

"Reluctantly, I left him, feeling as though leaving a friend so strongly had his quiet demeanor and forgiving spirit impressed me. In those few minutes I had, I did not know whether he died or lived for I could never find time to return to the spot, although wishing to do so, but often has my mind returned to that spot, surrounded by those scenes of duty which everywhere wet the eye in Shenandoah Valley, with the autumn sun sinking behind the mountains; and have felt at times when weary with the perplexities of life, almost envious of the quite repose of the soldier.

"It would gratify me to know if you receive this. Anything directed to Augusta, ME, care 'Maine Farmer' will reach me. I am, dear Sir, with great respect, Your obedient servant, LaGrange Severance"

Nov. 16, 1863
From Toronto, Canada
To his father in Stanton, Kentucky

Dear Pa,

Since my arrival at this place I have written you several letters but I have not been fortunate enough as yet, to receive any.

Doubtless, you have heard of my escape through my friends at Camp Douglas. I regard my escape from the 'Hades of the North' as the best thing I ever did in my lfe. The way and manner in which prisoners are treated at Camp Douglas is perfectly revolting to the mind of one who in other days, has been blessed and honored by the proud name of 'freeman.'

Well, I will tell you about my escape. The first time I ever attempted my escape I met with a miserable failure. Two others attempted to escape with me. We arranged it with two sentinels to jump over the prison walls at two o'clock A.M. We thought we had the thing 'fixed up' very nicely, indeed. At the appointed hour, we passed across the beat of the sentinels whom we had bribed, scaled the fence and had but a very short distance when we were surrounded by a host of Yankee scoundrels. We then found out that it was too late; that we had been basely betrayed. We were searched—all of our money was taken from us and, worse than all, we were hand-cuffed and thrown into a dungeon where I was kept closely confined for two weeks.

After my release I stayed in Camp Douglas until the ninth of Oct. when I bid adieu to my friends and concluded to take a pleasant trip to Canada. I found no difficulty, whatever in getting into a fine and lucrative business. I am clerking in one of the largest wholesale stores in this city. I expect to stay here until Spring. I intend to go over to Liverpool or London next May, get on a blockade runner, and go to Dixie. I have greater hopes for the success of our cause than I have ever had. Darkness has been turned into light. The bright sun of Liberty is just beginning to dawn in the Infant Confederacy....Our nation is bound together by the ties of patriotism.

You can tell the parents and friends of the boys who live in your neighborhood, that their sons and friends at Camp Douglas are all true. Unlike some cowards, wretched, faint-hearted dogs, they would die before they would take the oath of allegiance to support the miserable, rotten and corrupt Yankee government. They never speak of any one of our soldiers who have taken the Yankee oath, but with scorn and contempt.

We have been exceedingly fortunate. Only two of us have been wounded, viz. George Helm at Milton, and Liberty Russell at Greasy Creek; but they have recovered ere this from their wounds. I must close as I know you are tired of my letter. You may see me ere soon. I am listening every day to hear of Burnsides being driven from E. Tennessee and Kentucky. If Kentucky is reclaimed soon, I will then have the opportunity of going safely through the Yankee lines. I am impatient to rejoin the army. I know every one of Morgan's men are needed. I wish to strike a few more good blows for Liberty. I hope to hear from you soon....

Very truly,
Your son George Alcorn

Note: Twenty-three year-old Alcorn left Toronto for the Western States, contracted typhoid fever, and died in Austin, NV.

Union prisoner William B. Perkins wrote to his mother from Prison No. 5, Danville, VA, in 1864. He was later transferred to Andersonville Prison, GA, where he died of dysentery on July 26, 1864.

"You should feel a glow of pride that we are battling for our country's rights and our country's laws and that we were not so craven hearted when our nation was in danger and called us for ...to stand by and see her perish and lend no helping hand. In this great affliction which has befallen our land we must bear a part of the load if we would be worthy...do it without murmuring and with a cheerful heart...women of the revolution what glorious sacrifices they made. Things might be much worse. It is true I would prefer hot biscuit coffee beef steak & potatoes for the one I get here and to play checkers with one's nose for months isn't pleasant still it is much better than carrying a wooden leg or an empty coat sleeve about for life. If I hadn't been captured at Chickamauga I might have been killed or wounded at Mission Ridge as Billy Thatcher was. By the way do you know where Billy was wounded and how severely? I heard he was at home. He is an old messmate and I think a good deal of him.

"I don't think we will see much more active service for if we are exchanged this coming month we will not get back to the field again before the end of summer & fall campaigns and during the winter....I got four letters from you last week and replied. I read your letters over every day. They are worth their weight in gold. As long as I continue to get them I shall be (contented) and happy....My box has not come yet. I shall be proud of so good a mother and so rich a box when it comes.

"We are fortunate in having for commander of the post a most efficient and gentlemanly officer in the person of Major Moffet. We like him much. Dont fret about me for I am quite well. Give my love to all the folks and kiss Charlie for me. Your loving son W.B. Perkins Prison No. 5 Danville, Va. Care Genl. Winder Richmond, Va."

Confederate soldier John Sewell Anglin wrote to his family on November 27, 1861, from Camp Pickens, near Manassas, VA:

"Every day or so we hear the Band commence playing a sad burial tune very suddenly. We know then that some poor boy's spirit has departed and presently we see the "Band" gradually appearing from out of some companies street, followed by a small corp bearing the last remains of some poor soldier in a plain pine coffin; common uniform clothes. And in a few moments we see them gradually disappearing wending their way around a hill to the original forest, a short sad tune played slowly and the corpse is born into the grave there to remain until the resurrection of the dead. Well that is the only and last tribute of respect paid to the dead."

WE APPRECIATE
OUR SERVICEMEN
UNITED STATES
SAVINGS BONDS
25TH ANNIVERSARY
5c

1865 ★ 1965
SALVATION
ARMY
One hundred years of service
UNITED 5c STATES

CREDITS

Special acknowledgment is given the following contributors to this book:

DEDICATION: Mr. Frank, Post Master General

DESERT STORM:
Page 2 — President George H. Bush and Mrs. Bush: The Bettmann Archive; Page 3 — General Colin Powell: The Department of Defense photo; Page 4 — Students: Associated Press/Wide World photo (hereafter AP/ Wide World); Page 6 — Courtesy of Special Ed. Class at Hungerford School, Staten Island, NY; Page 7 — The Bettmann Archive; Page 8 — Photo and letter courtesy of Rochelle Lerch and MM3 Lonnie Van Dusen; Page 9 — AP/Wide World photo; Page 10 — © Rudi Frey/TIME Magazine photo; Page 11 — © Dennis Brack/TIME Magazine photo; Page 12 — © Dennis Brack/TIME Magazine photo; Page 14 — The Bettmann Archive ; Page 15 — AP/Wide World photo; Page 16 — Sgt. Garrison, Department of Defense photo; Page 17 — © Larry Downing, Woodfin Camp photo; Page 18 — © John Ficara, Woodfin Camp photo; Page 21 — © Rudi Frey/TIME Magazine photo; Page 24 — photo courtesy of Sgt. Doug Jarvis; Page 25 —Left, © Ed Bailey,and Right, USAF MSgt. Bill Thompson, Department of Defense photos; Page 26 — AP/Wide World photo; Page 27 — © Ed Bailey, Department of Defense photo; Page 31 © Ed Bailey, Department of Defense photo; Page 34 — Department of Defense photo; Page 35 — @ Terry Ashe, TIME Magazine photo; Page 36 — © John Ficara, Woodfin Camp photo; Page 37 — AP/Wide World photo; Page 39 — © Ed Bailey, Department of Defense photo; Page 41 — AP/Wide World photo; Page 42 — Left, The Bettmann Archive photo; Right, USAF MSgt. Bill Thompson,Department of Defense photo; Page 44 — Courtesy of Mrs. Ruth Murray; Page 45 — AP/Wide World photo; Page 48— AP/Wide World photo; Page 50 — AP/Wide World photo; Page 52 — © Ed Bailey, Department of Defense photo; Page 53 — AP/Wide World photo; Page 54 — Photo courtesy of Mr. and Mrs. Rolf Kruger and Sergeant and Mrs. Rogelio McLean, Page 55 — Photos courtesy of Daniel Feliciano and Danielle Gutierrez; Page 56— The Bettmann Archive photo; Page 57 — AP/Wide World photo; Page 59 — © Barry Iverson/TIME Magazine; Page 64 —Right, © Tsgt. Rose Reynolds and Left, Ed Bailey, Department of Defense photos; Page 65 — © John Ficara, Woodfin Camp photo; Page 66 — Truck photo courtesy of Chad Kornelis; Page 67 — AP/Wide World photo; Page 69 — Department of Defense; Page 70 — AP/Wide World photo; Page 72 – 73 — Photos and letter courtesy of Melanie D. Frank; Page 74 — Photo courtesy of Terry Rosta.

VIETNAM:
Page 78 — U.S. Army Military History Institute, Carlisle, PA photo; Page 80 — Photo and letter courtesy of Ann Younkins; Page 81 — Letter courtesy of Margaret Goodrich Hodge; AP/Wide World photo; Page 82 — Photos and letter courtesy of Clarence Coleman; Page 83 — Photo and letter courtesy of Jacques deRemer; Page 84 — Photo (left) The Bettmann Archive; photo and letter (right) courtesy of Vaughn Bartek; Page 85 — Photo and letter courtesy of Richard Bartek; Page 86 — (right) Illustrated envelope courtesy of Debra Sandau, (left) U.S. Army Military History Institute; Page 87 — Letter and photo courtesy of Lloyd L. Burke; Page 88 — Letter and photo courtesy of Katie Sutherland; Page 89 — © Larry Olsen, UNIPHOTO.

KOREA:
Page 92 — U.S. Army Military History Institute photo; Page 93 — Commemorative coin courtesy of the Korean War Veterans Association; Captain Norman Allan letter printed with permission from "The Korean War, Pusan to Chosen," by Donald Knox, published by Harcourt Brace Jovanovich, Inc.; Page 94 — Letter and covers courtesy of Louis C. Bakula; Page 95 — Letter and photo courtesy of James Cardinal; Page 96 — Letter and photos courtesy of Lloyd L. Burke; Page 9 7 — Letter and photo courtesy of Tommy E. McKinney; Page 98 — Letter and photo courtesy of Kathleen Cronan Wyosnick; Page 99 — Letter courtesy of Frederick P. Pelser: © Frank Noel, AP photo; Page 100 — (left) U.S. Army Military History Institute; (right) Letter and photo courtesy of Diane M. Dillon, sister of John Train; Page 101 — Letter and photo courtesy of Louis A. Eberhardt.

WORLD WAR II:
Page 104 — The Bettmann Archive photo; Page 105 — Letter from: "Letters to Mamie," by John S.D. Eisenhower, printed courtesy of DOUBLEDAY, a division of Bantam, Doubleday, Dell Publishing Group, Inc.© 1977-1978 by John S.D. Eisenhower and Mercantile Safe Deposit & Trust Company as Trustees for the Estate of Dwight D. Eisenhower, Page 106 — Photo courtesy of the National Archives; Page 107 — (left) Two letters courtesy of U.S. Army Military History Institute, photo courtesy of Howard J. Silbar; (right) courtesy of National Archives; Page 108 — Ernie Pyle dispatches from "Ernie's War," © David Nicholls, a Touchstone Book published by Simon & Schuster by arrangement with Random House, Inc., New York, 1986; Bill Mauldin art, reprint permission granted by Chicago Sun-Times, © Bill Mauldin; Page 109 — Photo and letter courtesy of Diane Dreher Klinkhammer; Page 110 — Photo and letters courtesy of John W. Drummond; Page 111 — Photo and letter courtesy of Eugene M. Maloney; Page 112 — Photo and letter courtesy of Bette Kamm Digby; Page 113 — Photos and letter and courtesy of Esther E. Shaffer; Page 114 — Photo and letter courtesy of U.S. Army Military History Institute; Page 115 — Photo and letter courtesy of U.S. Army Military History Institute; Page 116 — Photo courtesy of The Bettmann Archive; Page 117 — Photo and letters courtesy of Joseph T. McDonald; Page 118 — Letter from "Nimitz" by E. B. Potter, © 1976, E.B. Potter. Permission granted by U.S. Naval Institute, Annapolis, MD; Page 119 — Photo courtesy of the National Archives; Page 120 — (left) V-Mail letter courtesy of George Vercessi; (right) Photo courtesy of U.S. Army Military History Institute; Page 121 — V-Mail courtesy of U.S. Postal Service Historian.

WORLD WAR I:
Page 124 — Photo courtesy of U.S. Army Military History Institute, Page 125 — Art courtesy of Smithsonian Institution; General John J. Pershing letter courtesy of Library of Congress Manuscript Division (Pershing collection); Page 126 — photo courtesy of the National Archives; Page 127 — Photo upper left courtesy of U.S. Army Military History Institute; portrait and letter courtesy of Harriette Lee; Page 128 — Photo courtesy of U.S.

Army Military History Institute; letter courtesy of Smithsonian Institution Philatelic Collection; Page 129 — Poster art courtesy of Library of Congress; letter courtesy of Chris J. Flammang; Page 130 — Photo courtesy of the National Archives; letters reprinted with permission of Macmillan Publishing Company from BESS W. TRUMAN by Margaret Truman. Copyright © 1986 by Margaret Truman Daniel; Page 131 — Photo courtesy of Smithsonian Institution; Page 132 — Photo and letter courtesy of Arthur J. Barlow;
Page 133— Photo courtesy U.S. Army Military History Institute.

SPANISH AMERICAN WAR:
Page 136 — Battle of Manila Bay painting courtesy of Beverley R. Robinson Collection, U.S. Naval Academy's Halligan Hall,; Page 137 — Photo and letter courtesy of U.S. Naval History Museum, Annapolis, MD; Page 139 — Photo courtesy of Smithsonian Institution; Page 140 — Photo courtesy of the National Archives; letter courtesy of Theodore Roosevelt Collection, Houghton Library, Harvard University, Cambridge, MA; Page 141 — Painting courtesy of Library of Congress; Page 142 — Letter courtesy of U.S. Army Military History Institute; Page 143 — Photo and letter courtesy of Donald R. Christner; Page 144 — Photo and letter courtesy of Robert H. Hardnacke;Page 145 — Photo courtesy of Donald R. Christner.

THE CIVIL WAR:
Page 147— "John Brown's Body" by Stephen Vincent Benet: From Selected Works of Stephen Vincent Benet; Holt, Rinehart & Winston, Inc. © 1927-28 , by Stephen Vincent Benet, Copyright renewed, 1955-56, Rosemary Carr Benet, Reprinted by permission of Brandt & Brandt Literary Agents, Inc.; Page 150 — Monitor and Merrimac Battle, courtesy of The Art Collection of the Union League of Philadelphia, PA; Page 151 — Letter courtesy of Library of Congress Manuscript Division; Page 152 — Envelope cachet courtesy of the Smithsonian Institution; Page 153 — Letter courtesy of Beverly Mosby Coleman, Grandson of John Singleton Mosby; Photo © Brown Brothers; Page 154 — Abraham Lincoln letter courtesy of Huntington Museum, San Marino, CA; Frank Leslie's Illustrated News lithograph on page 155 courtesy of Fort Ward Museum, City of Alexandria, VA; Page 156 — Photo of General Robert E. Lee courtesy of the National Archives; letter from "ROBERT E. LEE, The Man and the Soldier" by Philip Van Doren Stern, 1963, courtesy of McGraw-Hill, Inc., New York; Page 157 — Watercolor painting by William Ludwell Sheppard courtesy of Eleanor S. Brockenborough Library, The Museum of the Confederacy, Richmond, VA; (photo by Katherine Wetzel); George F. Alverson letter courtesy of U.S. Army Military History Institute; Page 158 — Letter from Rufus and Douglass Cater Collection, Library of Congress Manuscript Division; photo courtesy of the Library of Congress; Page 159 — Letter courtesy of Sally M. Bennett; original letter in Holdridge, Nebraska Museum; Page 160 — Photo and letter courtesy of U.S.Army Military History Institute; Page 161 — Photo and letter courtesy of Aubrey F. Williams; Page 162 — Photo and letter courtesy of Colonel (Ret) Dean T. Vanderhoef and Paten Free Library, Bath, ME, publisher of "Now I Am a Soldier—the Civil War Diaries of Lorenzo Vanderhoef," editors Kenneth R. Martin and Ralph Linwood Snow, 1990; Page 163 — Photo courtesy of Library of Congress; Page 164 — Photo by U.S. Postal Service; letter courtesy of Fort Ward Museum, City of Alexandria, VA; Page 165 — Photo courtesy of U.S. Army Military History Institute; letter courtesy of Karyl Chastain Beal; Page 166 — Letter courtesy of Ellen L. Barnes;
Page 167 — Photo courtesy of the National Archives; letter courtesy of "The Confederate Philatelist" July-August, 1990; Page 168 — Letter courtesy of Library of Congress Manuscript Division; Charcoal drawing courtesy of Library of Congress.

ACKNOWLEDGEMENTS

The U.S. Postal Service thanks the following for prompt and courteous cooperation in providing research assistance and resources critical to a work of this magnitude: The Department of Defense; the U.S. Military History Institute, Carlisle, PA; the Library of Congress Manuscript Division; Mrs Rita Moroney, Historian Emeritus, Office of the Postmaster General; the staff of the U.S. Postal Service Headquarters Library; the Library of Congress Prints and Photographs Division; the National Archives; the Smithsonian Institution; the U.S. Naval Academy Museum at Annapolis, MD; the Fort Ward Museum of the City of Alexandria, VA; the Dudley Knox Center for Naval History, Washington, DC Navy Yard; the Huntington Library, San Marino, CA; the Bleyhl Community Library, Grandview, WA; the White House of the Confederacy, Richmond, VA; the Korean War Veterans Association; the American Legion; the Veterans of Foreign Wars; the Friends of the Vietnam Memorial; Associated Press (AP); Universal Press International (UPI); Reuters; TIME Magazine; the Chicago Sun-Times; and the book publishers whose reprint rights appear on the credits pages.

To the many thoughtful persons who sent in letters not included in this book, our heartfelt thanks. It was difficult to make a selection, for many letters expressed similar thoughts and messages. The fact that some were not chosen does not diminish their importance, for each letter had special significance to both sender and recipient.

Special thanks are extended to the U.S. Postal Service Headquarters telephone operators and postal employees throughout the nation. They provided invaluable assistance in locating authors and families whose letters appear in this book. Successful completion of the task depended upon their expertise and involvement.

Deborah K. Bowker and Azeezaly S. Jaffer for program management;
Frank P. Brennan Jr., for project direction;
James Adams, for project management
Jeanne O'Neill and Bill Olcheski for editing, research and narrative material;
Jane Bush for visual research;
Thad E. Dilley for creative direction, design, photo editing and production quality control;
Nancy Van Meter for graphic design, typesetting and art production;
Lee Roberts for print production;
Gregrick A. Frey for research assistance;
Kelly M. O'Brien and Lisa Wellington for letters research assistance;
Jean Davis-Smith for proofreading;
Young & Rubicam Inc./CYB. Yasumura for cover design; Bettman Archive/ Bettman Newsphotos/Ried Rossman for cover photo.